When "I Love You" Turns
Violent

Abuse in Dating Relationships

When "I Love You" Turns

Violent

Abuse in Dating
Relationships

Scott A. Johnson

NEW HORIZON PRESS
Far Hills, New Jersey

Copyright Acknowledgments

The author and publisher gratefully acknowledge permission to use the following materials:

Figure 1 is adapted from the Power and Control Wheel, Domestic Abuse Intervention Project, Duluth, MN. Used with permission.

Portions of Appendix VI are adapted from material by the Family Violence Network, Lake Elmo, MN. Used with permission.

Library of Congress Catalog Card Number: 92-63127

Johnson, Scott A.
    When "I love you" turns violent: Abuse in dating relationships

ISBN: 0-88282-124-5
New Horizon Press

Manufactured in the U.S.A.

1997 1996 1995 1994 1993 / 5 4 3 2 1

Contents

Contents

Figures

CHAPTER ONE

Defining Violence

David and Sarah have been dating for two months. Her friends have noticed that she spends less time with them, avoids looking anyone in the eye, and on occasion has bruises on her arms and face. She quickly explains that she is clumsy, "and sometimes David gets a little angry." Her friends express concern about Sarah being abused, but Sarah refuses to listen. That night she and David go out to dinner, and she tells him about her conversation with her friends and how they expressed concern about the dating relationship.

David insists that they continue the conversation at his apartment, and without any discussion he drives her to his home. Inside, David grabs Sarah by the arm, pushes her onto the couch, and begins to yell. "You had no business talking to anyone about me! I have never treated you mean!" He proceeds to take his pants off and tells Sarah she had better have sex with him "because you belong to me." David forces Sarah to have sex, and in the process he leaves several bruises on her arms, legs, and chest. After finishing the act, David tells Sarah that he loves her and that he would never do anything to hurt her.

Examples of abuse such as this one are increasing. Unfortunately, most victims of dating violence cannot accept the fact that they are victims. Often someone outside the relationship is the first to correctly label the relationship as abusive, long before the victim or the abuser realizes it. This occurs because of the fear, confusion, and pain victims experience. No one likes to admit that they have been a victim of any kind of violence, let alone violent suffered at the hands of someone close and dear. However, with dating violence increasing daily, it is imperative that we educate ourselves about this form of violence.

Our society is relationship orientated. We are social beings by nature. To be happy involves having a partner or a significant other with whom to share our lives. Despite our tendency to socialize and develop relationships with others, however, many of us have not yet learned how to get along with others, nor have we learned how to build and maintain healthy relationships. As we desperately seek to find that special someone to date and eventually marry or make our life partner, we find that we have no guide to tell us when we have found the right person or how to behave toward them.

We place enormous value on education. Today even many menial jobs require a high school diploma. We often spend years at college or graduate school to achieve certain positions; yet we are never directly taught how to fulfill the various roles we play in our personal lives, such as friend, girlfriend or boyfriend, significant other or partner, mother or father, husband or wife. We learn such roles mostly through observing and modeling our behavior after the behavior of others. The problem here is inherent, for those we observe learned by observing others, and so on. Often it is a classic case of the blind leading the blind.

It is little wonder then that we so often hear about child abuse and domestic abuse. We are beginning to accept the fact that violence does occur between married people and to children, but most of us remain ignorant that apart from date rape—which has received attention recently—many other types of abuse occur.

When I lecture in high schools, the students often begin our discussion believing that abuse rarely happens in their dating relationships. Even as I answer their preliminary questions about what the definitions of abuse are, only a few students label their relationships as abusive. However, after I give examples of the varied types of abuse, over 85 percent of the students state that they have been, are being, or know of a friend being abused! It is frightening that between the ages of fifteen and eighteen, most young people have already experienced dating abuse in some way. I have found that the statistics are not much different for adults and college students.

What, then, is abuse?

Abuse refers to any act that is intended to cause or results in harm to another person. Included here are verbal put-downs and name calling on one extreme, to pushing, slapping, rape, and murder on the other extreme.

Harm is the emotional, psychological, physical, or sexual injury that occurs as a result of abuse. We may not always be able to see that abuse has occurred. There may be no scars, bruises, or bleeding; nevertheless, other factors and symptoms are present.

Intent refers to what a person wants to do—the plan. The concept of intent often causes confusion, and it is often believed that abusers do not intend or mean to cause harm. But all abuse is planned, and when abuse occurs it is because of a conscious choice made by the abuser. Abusers make a decision; they give themselves permission to abuse. Intent may be difficult to establish or prove, but if the goal is to create fear, injury, or to gain the cooperation of someone through intimidation, force, or injury, then abuse is intentional. Often abusers claim that the abuse was an accident. Accidents do occur, but *abuse toward one's significant other is always a planned choice.* It never occurs by chance.

As to frequency, whether the abusive act occurs only once or several times, it is still abuse. Too often abusers claim that they did not "mean" to or "intend" to cause harm or be abusive; but abuse is always a conscious choice, and therefore intent is

3

implied. The fact that the majority of abusers tend to abuse only a selected few people indicates that a choice is being made—a choice that includes a conscious effort to evaluate situations and adjust how they behave toward others. Toward some the abuser may behave in a kind and respectful manner, while behaving disrespectfully toward others. The terms *abuse* and *violence* will be used interchangeably throughout this book.

There are four types of abuse: *emotional, psychological, physical,* and *sexual.*

Emotional Abuse

Frank tells Pam that she is not capable of doing anything right. When she does something for him, Frank usually finds something to criticize. Pam finally tells Frank that she is leaving the relationship, and Frank says, "Leaving me proves that you always run away when you fail."

Also referred to as verbal abuse, emotional abuse refers to the attacking of someone's self-worth and self-esteem. Emotional abuse makes the victim feel degraded, uneasy, confused, and angry. Examples of emotional abuse include name calling, putdowns, belittling of accomplishments, and swearing. This is the most common form of abuse, and usually it is present in all other types of abuse. Often people overlook emotional abuse and may accept it as normal behavior. However, it *is* a type of abuse. In most cases the abuser will eventually progress to abusing the significant other in other ways, the abuse becoming increasingly severe.

Emotional abuse marks the beginning of an abusive relationship and should be taken just as seriously as psychological, physical, and sexual abuse.

Psychological Abuse

Scott refers to Jean as stupid. He threatens to harm her and then contradicts himself, blaming her for hearing him wrong, in an effort to make Jean appear crazy. When Jean completes her college degree, Scott calls her a "dummy" and belittles her degree as being "easy to get if you got one." Scott prioritizes everyone and everything before Jean. When Jean ends the relationship, Scott blames her for all of the problems they had.

Psychological abuse refers to the attacking of someone's self-esteem and self-worth, but the attacks are made against the whole being of the other person. Examples include:

- threatening to harm the other,
- threatening to or actually destroying the other's belongings,
- hitting or destroying property (doors, walls, chairs, pictures, and so on),
- threatening to or actually taking or harming the children,
- monitoring the other's actions (who they talk to, where they go, who they see, and so on),
- withholding and/or controlling the other's money, including taking money and making the other buy things for the abuser,
- verbal attacks and name calling,
- interrupting eating and/or sleeping patterns,
- forcing the other to do anything degrading, humiliating, or dangerous,
- criticizing the other's thoughts, beliefs, or behaviors,
- belittling the other's accomplishments,
- treating the other as if inferior or a servant,
- acting jealous, possessive, "guarding" the other.

As a result of psychological abuse, the victim may experience fear—of the abuser, of being harmed, or of others finding out about the abuse—as well as feelings of being trapped, worthless, and exploited.

Psychological abuse involves *objectification*. This occurs when abusers begin to view their significant others as possessions, objects they own, rather than people. Objectifying their significant others makes it easier for abusers to abuse. It is much easier to abuse an object than a person. Name calling and jealousy are part of objectification. The abuser who psychologically abuses his or her significant other will eventually progress to physical and sexual abuse.

Although many people differentiate between emotional and psychological abuse, the differences are small. Both emotional and psychological abuse are attacks upon a person's identity, self-esteem, and self-worth, and both are abuse. On a scale of severity, these two rank on the bottom, but the effects are often more devastating and long-lasting than other forms of abuse.

Physical Abuse

Kathy pinches and slaps Ted when she becomes angry. Ted attempts to calm her down, but his attempts only seem to exacerbate Kathy's rage. Kathy punches him in the eye, which turns black and blue. Ted cannot find a way to tell anyone, and he feels trapped.

Reggie is jealous of Samantha. He often feels insecure and blames his feelings on her supposedly seeing other men. Reggie threatens that if she ever cheated on him, he would cut her "so that nobody would ever want you." Reggie slaps Samantha across the face, grabs her by the hair, and slams her against the wall.

Physical abuse involves physical attacks, including any unwanted bodily contact. Common examples include:

- slapping
- punching
- pushing
- kicking
- grabbing
- choking
- throwing objects
- spanking
- wrestling
- pinching
- biting
- choking
- spitting
- scratching
- throwing the other bodily
- burning
- pulling hair
- restraining (holding the other down, not allowing them to leave, etc.)
- using any object or weapon against the other (including a stick, belt, paddle, whip, rope, knife, gun, or any object that can cause injury or be used to create fear through threatening to use or actually using the object).

Emotional and psychological abuse are inherently involved in physical abuse. However, during physical abuse the immediate safety of the victim is in jeopardy. When abusers have progressed to using physical abuse, they have totally objectified their significant others. What this means is that such victims are viewed as possessions, owned by the abusers. The abuser believes that he or she owns the significant other, just as one owns a car. It is always easier to physically attack an object than another human being.

Sexual Abuse

Alex smooth-talks Greta into making out. He promises to only touch her. After several minutes of touching, Alex begins to get rough. He gets on top of Greta, takes off his pants, and forces her to have oral sex. He then blames her by saying, "You got me so turned on that I couldn't stop"—which was his plan all along.

Tammy pressures Harry into sexual intercourse. Harry explains that he is tired and not in the mood. He also says that until their relationship deepens, he is not comfortable having intercourse with her. Tammy begins to rub Harry's crotch, pleading him to have sex with her. She asks him, "What kind of man are you that you don't want to have sex with me? What's wrong with you?" He then complies with her demands out of feelings of guilt, shame, and helplessness—he does not want to end his relationship with her.

Greg dances with Paul at the bar. As they dance, Greg begins to rub Paul's butt and thighs. Paul removes Greg's hands and tells him to stop. Greg becomes enraged, calls Paul a "bitch," grabs him by the arm and takes him to the back of the bar. Greg tells Paul, "I bought you drinks, I danced with you, and you owe me sex. Prove that you care about me." Paul feels obligated to do as Greg says.

Sexual abuse involves attacking someone sexually. This includes any forced sexual contact, whether by coercion (psychological force), physical force, threats, or ignoring the other's rights and requests. Examples include:

- unwanted sexual comments or gestures,
- touching the other sexually without consent,
- forcing the other to commit any sexual act against his or her will, including having sex with others, videotaping, the use of objects, and so on,

- ignoring the other's "no's,"
- pushing or breaking sexual limits or boundaries,
- intimidating, begging, or using love as a means of forcing sexual contact ("Prove that you love me"),
- engaging in sexual activity when the other is impaired (sleeping, injured, under the influence of drugs or alcohol) or unable to say no for any reason (does not speak same language, hearing/speech impairment).

Sexual abuse also includes all other types of abuse because physical contact is made, and emotional and psychological abuse are involved. Sexual abuse is *rape*. Sexual abuse is an extremely intricate and complicated topic, and for the purpose at hand will be dealt with only as it relates to violence within dating relationships.

Victim refers to the person upon whom the violence/abuse is directed. *Abuser* and *perpetrator* refer to the person committing the abuse, and these terms may be used interchangeably. *Significant other*, *date*, and *partner* refer to the person with whom the abuser is involved in a dating relationship.

One last distinction will be made. When putting a label on abuse, the type of relationship is taken into account. There are three common labels: domestic violence, child abuse, and dating violence. *Domestic violence* refers to abuse occurring within a marriage. Sometimes this term also includes people who are engaged to be married or are living together regardless of marital status, especially when used in legal terms. *Child abuse* refers to an adult's violence toward a child. *Dating violence* refers to abuse occurring within a dating relationship. This involves any dating relationship, regardless of sexual orientation or age.

One dating couple I counseled whose relationship had violent aspects was John and Betty. Prior to our session together, John was arrested for physically abusing Betty. When he came in for his initial assessment he greatly minimized his abusive behavior and apologized to Betty if he had hurt her with his yelling and pushing. John made it clear to Betty and me that he never intended to hurt Betty, or anyone for that matter. He stated that when things did not go his way, and if he was under stress, he could not control his temper. For several sessions John described how he believed he was powerless over his anger and how he was out of control.

Interestingly, Betty told a different story about John's "powerlessness." She explained that he would be very quiet when something was bothering him, and he would distance himself from everyone by keeping a mean and intimidating look on his face. She further described how John would yell at her for anything she did, and when she asked him what was wrong, he would become increasingly agitated and angry. Sometimes John would go off by himself, go to his parents, or hang out with his friends, and when he returned to spend time with Betty he would be calm.

Betty further described how John behaved if he did not leave when he was angry and stressed. He would first appear to pick a fight with her by not leaving her alone and would become more blaming and paranoid as she tried to calm him. At times, he would end up apologizing to her and giving her a hug, after which he would talk about what was bothering him. Other times, however, John became a different man. He threatened to have affairs and also threatened to hurt her. John had slapped Betty, pushed her against the wall, and forced her to have sex with him.

When John listened to Betty's description of how he behaved, he first became angry, denying her observations. He blamed her for not listening to him, for being selfish, and for not meeting his needs. After some time in therapy, John broke down and cried. I asked him what was wrong, and he replied that Betty's assessments were right. He could not believe that he could treat Betty, or anyone for that matter, in such an abusive manner. John's abusive behaviors were traumatic for both of them.

During our sessions John recognized that only he could give himself permission to hurt Betty and that when he gave himself permission to be "out of control" he was actually in total control. John began to realize that by making the decision to abuse Betty, he blatantly intended to cause her harm.

Unfortunately, this type of abuse is prevalent. Violence within dating relationships is nothing new; rather, there is a new focus on it. It would be simplistic to believe that abuse only occurs within marriage or between parents and children. Abuse is pervasive throughout our society and has presented us with a serious chronic problem that, left untreated, will infect the quality of all our relationships.

CHAPTER TWO

The Forms of Abuse

There are ten different forms of abuse (see Figure 1). There is much overlap among these forms of abuse, and at times it is difficult to distinguish between them. When abuse is occurring, it most often involves more than one form of abuse.

Intimidation

Peter often tells Marsha's friends that she is unfaithful to him, and he tells everyone that they are having sex when in fact Marsha has refused to be sexual with him. Peter occasionally yells at her and physically blocks the door to prevent Marsha from leaving. This is intimidation, and it creates significant fear for the victim. As a result, Marsha often complies with his demands for forced sexual contact and is subsequently raped.

Intimidation occurs when the abuser instills fear in his or her victim. The abuser does this through looks, stares, or glances, by focusing attention on the victim, and so on. Intimidation may take the form of gestures, which may include raising the arm or

Figure 1. The Abuse Chart.

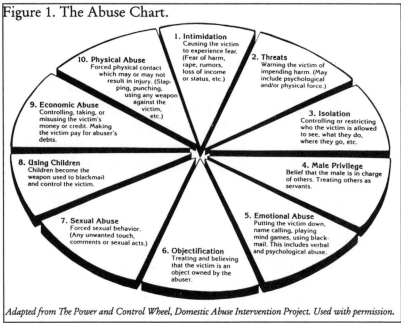

1. **Intimidation**
Causing the victim to experience fear. (Fear of harm, rape, rumors, loss of income or status, etc.)

2. **Threats**
Warning the victim of impending harm. (May include psychological and/or physical force.)

3. **Isolation**
Controlling or restricting who the victim is allowed to see, what they do, where they go, etc.

4. **Male Privilege**
Belief that the male is in charge of others. Treating others as servants.

5. **Emotional Abuse**
Putting the victim down, name calling, playing mind games, using blackmail. This includes verbal and psychological abuse.

6. **Objectification**
Treating and believing that the victim is an object owned by the abuser.

7. **Sexual Abuse**
Forced sexual behavior. (Any unwanted touch, comments or sexual acts.)

8. **Using Children**
Children become the weapon used to blackmail and control the victim.

9. **Economic Abuse**
Controlling, taking, or misusing the victim's money or credit. Making the victim pay for abuser's debts.

10. **Physical Abuse**
Forced physical contact which may or may not result in injury. (Slapping, punching, using any weapon against the victim, etc.)

Adapted from The Power and Control Wheel, Domestic Abuse Intervention Project. Used with permission.

leg as if to hit or kick, making a fist, holding an object as if ready to throw, break, or hit with it, as well as using a loud voice and yelling.

Intimidating actions include any behavior intended to create fear, such as walking threateningly toward someone, punching one's own fist into the wall, kicking something such as a table or door, slamming a door, tearing a phone from the wall, and so on. Holding a weapon, even if not threatening to use it, is also a form of intimidation. Physical size and posture may also be used to intimidate a person. Intimidation is the abuser's way of letting the victim know that he or she is in control and that psychological and physical force may be used if the victim refuses to cooperate with the abuser's demands.

◆   ◆   ◆

Threats

Susan wants Henry to give her fine jewelry and has told him to buy the gifts for her or she will have an affair. Susan states that if Henry refuses, she may tell his parents that he abuses her.

Threats, whether of physical, sexual, or psychological harm, create fear for the victim. Threats are a direct verbal or nonverbal statement that if one fails to do as told, consequences and harm will occur.

Threats are closely related to intimidation, and at times it is impossible to tell the difference between them. Threats include actually giving verbal or physical warning to the victim of impending harm, that is, letting the victim know that the abuser will harm them if he or she does not do as the abuser says. The harm may be directed toward the victim or others and may include threats to damage or destroy property or to injure children or pets.

Often threats include spreading vicious rumors or even telling others personal truths that may emotionally harm the victim. Examples may include telling lies (or the truth) about sexual preference, faithfulness, criminal behavior or history, parenting skills, mental health problems, and medical problems.

Often abusers threaten to commit suicide, or, in extreme cases, to murder their victims. Although threats of either suicide or homicide need to be taken seriously, in most cases the abuser cares about him- or herself far too much to harm themselves, and most often needs the victim to continue in that role far too much to fatally wound him or her. However, if the abuser chooses suicide, it is his or her own choice, and only qualified mental health professionals may help such a person. The best thing to do with someone who threatens suicide is to encourage that person to seek counseling. The responsibility of choosing suicide rests with the person threatening to harm him- or herself. No one else is ever to blame for a suicide's morbid choice of acts.

Because it is difficult to identify which abusers will follow through with their threats, if an abuser threatens a person's life, the threats should be taken very seriously. Police protection is one of the few tools victims may have to protect themselves. Also, when an abuser is threatening to kill, he or she has progressed to the end of the violence continuum and is not likely to change. Professional intervention is warranted.

Isolation

Carol and Beth have been dating for several months. Carol becomes jealous of Beth's friends and demands that Beth run all plans through Carol and get permission. Carol has even sabotaged Beth's plans and expects that Beth will spend all of her time with her. Isolation effectively cuts off any source of support for the victim and allows only a distorted sense of reality for the victim to compare their relationship with.

Isolation often occurs in abusive relationships and can be an important force preventing a victim from seeking help and assistance. Isolation includes controlling who a victim sees and talks to, what he or she does, and where he or she goes. When an abuser prevents the victim from seeing another person, the abuser has effectively prevented the victim from gaining the support necessary to aid in leaving the abuser or ending the relationship. If the abuser prevents the victim from attending school or work, the victim may lose self-esteem, as well as the sense of accomplishment that comes from attaining goals. The abuser may actually feel threatened if the victim attains a college or graduate degree, believing that the victim may become more intelligent and knowledgeable than the abuser and may be better able to leave the relationship and survive.

Isolation scars and at times can lead to lasting emotional damage because it leads the victim to feeling helpless, alone, and trapped. Being isolated also increases the chance of the victim believing that abuse is a natural, accepted form of expression because there may not be access to healthy relationships with which to compare their current relationship. Isolation may also increase the victim's belief that the abuse is his or her own fault, that somehow the abuse is deserved (which is *never* the case).

Male Privilege

Willy expects Ellen to meet any demand he makes, to wait at home for his call, and to never question him. Willy believes that men are in charge of any relationship and that using any force or violence toward someone refusing their requests is acceptable. The male privilege is a form of bigotry and is sometimes used my men to justify child abuse and sexual assault.

"Male privilege" is the belief that males are in charge, not only of decisions within relationships, but also in their significant others' lives, bodies, and futures. The best example is that of a servant-master relationship. The servant is not allowed to voice his or her opinions, wants, or dislikes, but rather is expected to do whatever he or she is told to do.

Often abusers who exercise the male privilege are openly and outwardly bigoted, and this may be directed toward other races, religions, political beliefs, and sexual orientations.

Certain people still hold strongly to such beliefs. Some countries continue to support male domination in relationships, which often results in females feeling like second-class citizens, disrespected and trapped by society.

Emotional Abuse

Chad and Mike spend much of their time together. Mike often puts Chad down by belittling his strengths and by telling Chad he is worthless without Mike. Emotional abuse destroys the victim's self-esteem, sense of worth, and sense of reality. As a result of being emotionally abused, Chad often doubts his sanity and worth.

Emotional abuse includes both verbal and psychological abuse. It refers to put-downs, name calling, objectifying, and mind games. Put-downs and name calling occur very often in abusive relationships and include words and phrases such as "You're no good," "You're a loser," "You're worthless," "Who would want you?" as well as vulgar names. Mind games occur when abusers attempt to make their significant others doubt their own identities or sanity, as well as taking advantage of emotional sore spots, such as bad past experiences (rape, death, mugging, divorce, miscarriage). Abusers may cause their significant others to feel guilty for refusing their requests. Another type of mind game may include statements that result in the victims doubting whether they are "normal," statements such as "Everyone else can do this, why can't you?" and "I'll have to find someone who can please me if you can't or won't."

Objectification

Steve views women as pieces of meat and usually refers to women as "sluts," "bitches," or "slaves." When Michelle went out on a date with him, he became angry when she talked with others and treated her as if he owned her. Objectification steals the victim's identity, self-worth, and freedom. Sexualization is a form of objectification, but the focus is on the sexuality and sexual parts of the person. Steve rarely finds a woman worthwhile unless she is complying with his demands, has an attractive body, or dresses in a fashion which emphasizes her breasts or legs. Unfortunately, Steve finds little to respect in women. Even if Michelle gives in to his demands, he will dump her after he gets what he wants.

Objectification is a key concept in any and all types and forms of abuse. Included here is treating one's significant other as an object that is owned, a prize of some sort. Common examples indicating objectification include name calling and sexualization. Sexualization is the same as objectification, but the focus is on the sexual appearance or sexual body parts of a person.

Objectifying is often used in times of war. We rename the enemy to make it easier to kill, because it is far easier to kill an object than a person. In dating violence (as well as in domestic violence) the abuser renames the victim, thereby allowing easier rationalization and justification for the abuse. That is why we often hear name calling prior to actual physical or sexual abuse. During the escalation phase, vulgar names serve to objectify the victim. When abusers call their significant others by vulgar, degrading names, less energy is required to abuse them because they are no longer viewed as human, but rather as objects.

Sexual Abuse

David and Shelly have been friends for a while, and have decided to have a date. As they arrive at David's home, they begin to drink alcohol and watch a romantic movie. David suggests that they go on a tour of the house. When David gets to his bedroom he coerces her to sit on the bed. He then forces himself on her and begins to engage in fondling and then oral sex. She refuses to participate and is shocked that David would treat her with such disrespect and force. David explains to Shelly that she owed him sex, and that if she did not want to have sex she would never have agreed to go out with him and definitely would not have gone to his bedroom. Sexual abuse is confusing, often catching the victim off guard and rendering him or her less capable of fighting off the attack.

Sexual abuse refers to any unwanted touch, comments, or forced sexual acts. A common form of sexual abuse within a dating relationship is treating one's significant other as a sex object. This would include physically forcing or coercing (talking the person into having sex, threatening, making the date feel guilty) someone into having any type of sexual activity including oral, anal, or vaginal penetration, use of objects, and having sex with others.

Obsessively focusing on sex when together is a sign of objectifying someone sexually; the victim becomes the abuser's sex object. It is important here to remember that we never love objects as we do people, and object love will never strengthen any relationship. When one person is obsessively focused on sex and the other is not interested in engaging in any sexual act, this can easily lead to abuse.

Males sometimes try to coerce their dating partners into having sex using as a rational the belief a man loses control after a certain point and must have sex when he becomes sexually aroused. Study after study has disproved this belief; it is a myth. There is no such thing as "a point of no return," only a point at which one is more likely to "give in" to the sexual act.

If your significant other cannot listen to and honor your requests to stop being sexual, then he or she does not care about you. Love demands respect. If a person cannot cope with sexual frustration, then he or she probably cannot cope with other forms of frustration and is in need of therapy to develop more effective coping skills. Remember, love demands respect, flexibility, and fairness. Talking, pressuring, or forcing a significant other into having sex is only succeeding at taking away part of his or her identity—that is, the person's ownership of his or her own body and therefore part of who that person really is.

Using Children

Floyd has been separated from his wife Donna for two months. When Floyd spends time with their children, he often questions them about their mother and puts her down in front of them. When Donna confronts him about his conduct, he threatens to withhold child support payments and even to cancel special events he had planned with the children. Using children as pawns of revenge to cause discomfort in anyone is not only abusive but repulsive. Any time children are used in this fashion, visitation with the children should be ceased.

Misusing children occurs when one or both persons in a relationship are parents and one uses the children to create fear or guilt in order to gain the cooperation of the other. Common examples include threatening to harm a significant other in the children's presence or threatening to harm the children. Attempting to turn a child against his or her parent or telling the child bad things about the parent are also forms of abuse. Threatening to tell family, friends, or the authorities that a significant other is a bad parent or has molested the child when this is untrue is also abuse.

21

When a couple has had a child together but one person attempts to terminate the relationship, an abuser may use the child to try to trap the victim into remaining in the relationship. This occurs when the abuser threatens to get custody of the child (without regard for the child's well-being), requests unreasonable visitations with the child, or refuses to make child support payments. The abuser is counting on the victim's feeling guilty about the abuser's situation to increase the chance the victim will be trapped into remaining in the relationship. An abuser may even attempt to make the other parent appear unfit to have custody of the child. This creates fear in the victim, and he or she may choose to remain in the relationship for fear of losing the child. This is abuse, and although it would be rare for an abuser to actually win custody of the child using such base methods, this does occur. When abusers use children to abuse their significant others, they are ruthless and do not care for or love anybody other than themselves.

Economic Abuse

Jan expects Paul to spend much of his money on her and sometimes gets angry when he does not spend as much as she wants. She punishes him by refusing dates and sex when he does not do as she demands.

Rick demands that Angie pay for his fun and often uses her charge cards and expects that she should pay. When she tells him that she cannot afford to pay his bills, he becomes angry and blackmails her into paying by threatening to end the relationship, thereby taking with him all the things that he charged on her credit cards.

Economic abuse was once thought to only occur in marriages. Only recently have we begun to understand that economic abuse is very common in dating relationships. It results in the victim losing a sense of control, happiness, and responsibility that making money can bring.

Economic abuse refers to controlling a significant other's money, such as by preventing him or her from attaining or maintaining employment, taking their money, or misusing the victim's credit cards. Making one's significant other pay for one's bills or making the victim ask for his or her own money is wrong. Adults do not receive an allowance and have the right to refuse to spend money on their significant others without needing an excuse.

Physical Abuse

Jack slaps Wendy when she refuses to do what he wants. He has even choked her when another male smiled at her. Phil puts Abe down a lot and has grabbed him by the hair and punched him when angry. Both Jack and Phil have something in common—they both use violence when hurt, frustrated, or angry.

Any physical abuse is bad, but there are differing degrees and severities of physical abuse. On one hand, we see pushing, slapping, and tripping; on the other hand are punching, kicking, raping, and using a weapon. Any form of physical violence is serious and unjustified. Regardless of the degree of severity, any form of physical abuse is dangerous and will become increasingly severe over time unless the abuser gets into therapy.

Physical—and sometimes sexual—abuse differs from other forms of abuse in that it can and does result in serious injury and even death. An extreme example is the nightclub fire in New York, set by an irate abusive man who wanted to teach his former girlfriend a lesson by burning down the nightclub she visited.

The result was that more than eighty people were killed and many others were seriously injured. There is never justification for the stupidity of violence, and in the end many innocent people may be affected.

One couple I counseled, Sheryl and Greg, had been dating for several months. They came to me at the request of a college counseling center to deal with what appeared to be abusive tendencies in the way they treated each other. They had hopes of marrying each other and were disturbed at how often they argued. It was determined that there had not been any threat of or actual physical abuse.

Greg admitted to being overly demanding of Sheryl's time. "I become jealous when other men show an interest in her," he said. Sheryl pointed out, "He makes it a point to make sure that whatever man I am talking with knows we are a couple. Greg comes up to them, puts his arm around me, and passionately kisses me." He would then introduce himself as Sheryl's boyfriend and not leave them alone. Sheryl would become annoyed and eventually angry that Greg did not trust her. She would then refuse to have sex with Greg. Greg responded by calling her a tease and accusing her of having sex with other men.

What became painfully obvious was that their relationship lacked trust, and both had serious unresolved issues that had not been identified or explored. Greg recalled being physically abused by his father and that his mother would often justify the abuse by blaming it on Greg's lack of commitment to the family. His parents rarely spent time with him, and when they did they usually broke any promises made to him. Sheryl's family was not physically abusive, but it lacked emotional intimacy. Her parents constantly criticized her and were never satisfied with her accomplishments, despite the fact that she was a straight-A student heading for a good career.

Because of their history of childhood abuse, Greg and Sheryl both learned a traumatic lesson: when they trusted the people they were supposed to (their parents), they were let down. As a result, neither could become emotionally intimate with anyone without expecting to be let down. When they were not let down, both sabotaged the relationship to justify arguing, which served the purpose of preventing them from developing an emotionally deeper relationship. Neither was able to open up to the other about his or her problems, and neither could risk being vulnerable to the other.

Their communication was usually superficial. Each wanted to love the other, but both lacked the skills to let their guard down long enough to risk trusting. Just as their parents had used several forms of abuse on them, they in turn began to abuse each other. Greg's abuse of Sheryl took the forms of objectifying, emotional abuse, jealousy, and the use of male privilege. Sheryl's abuse of Greg took the form of emotional and sexual abuse (by withholding sex as punishment).

Abusive behavior is one of many means used for achieving power and control over another person. I am not implying that power and control are always bad, because we cannot survive without a sufficient amount of both in our lives. However, when the end result or purpose is to abuse, hurt, or not respect someone, then such behavior is unhealthy and wrong.

To repeat the axiom: If you are being abused, your significant other is telling you loud and clear, *"I do not love you!"*

CHAPTER THREE

The Abuse Cycle

Violence within any relationship, especially a dating relationship, is a complex pattern of behaviors. The *abuse cycle* adapted from Lenore Walker illustrates this pattern very well. There are three stages that make up the abuse cycle: *escalation, explosion,* and *honeymoon.* Each stage involves distinct behaviors. It is important to understand the abuse cycle in order to recognize, prevent, and treat abuse (see Figure 2).

The Escalation Stage

Doug gets home from work and tells Heidi that she'd better leave him alone. He paces the room, grabs a beer, and yells at Heidi to get him something to eat. Heidi asks what is wrong and tries to give him a hug. Doug begins to think in distorted ways and blames her for his bad day. Heidi recognizes Doug's escalation and chooses to leave him alone, realizing that he will not hear anything she has to say. She has seen him act this way before.

When Sam talks with Karen, she becomes irritable and focuses only on a single point. Karen raises her voice, crosses her arms,

Figure 2. The Three Stages of the Abusive Relationship.

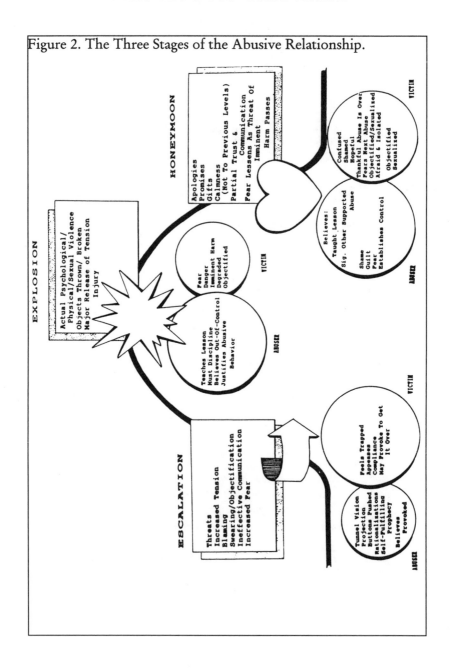

and makes intense eye contact with Sam. Sam cannot understand what is happening. When he asks her to stop yelling for a moment, Karen becomes defensive and storms out of the room. Sam noticed that Karen was escalating and attempted to settle the situation down to calmly discuss the problem at hand.

The escalation stage refers to the buildup of tension and marks the beginning of the abuse cycle. Verbal and psychological abuse occur, with the bulk of the blame being placed on the victim. This is the most important stage to understand, because recognizing when the cycle is beginning offers the opportunity to leave the situation or take a time-out. There are indicators of impending abuse, and these warn that abuse is about to happen. There are five cue areas of focus: *situations* (including "buttons"), *thoughts* (cognitions), *emotional, physical and behavioral,* and *red flag words and phrases.*

Situations

There are usually specific situations and issues the abuser has difficulty coping with. When these are mentioned or discussed, regardless of whether the victim or abuser brings them up, the abuser begins the abuse cycle by escalating.

Common situations or topics include faithfulness, sexual behavior, and relationship and personal growth issues. It is not the issues discussed that cause abuse to occur, but rather the abuser's inability or unwillingness to deal with these issues or situations appropriately. The abuser becomes frustrated and angry when he or she has to deal with these problems. Most abusers have a very low tolerance of frustration, and this is referred to as Low Frustration Tolerance (LFT) and will be discussed in more detail in Chapter 4.

LFT basically means that the abuser tends to get overly excited or upset when frustrated and as a result will often choose extreme emotional and behavioral responses. For example, instead of feeling annoyed that someone is in front of him in a line, an abuser could become angry and possibly curse or punch them.

Thoughts and Cognitions

Thoughts and cognitions refer to the beliefs we hold and the process by which we evaluate the events or situations we experience. Basically we decide how to respond to the event or situation and what it means. Then we use our evaluation of the events to decide which emotion and behavior seems appropriate to express. During the escalation stage, abusers need to find some rationale or reason to allow themselves to abuse their significant others.

Common examples include abusers telling themselves that their victims behaved in an unacceptable manner and as a result should be punished or taught a lesson. Statements such as "You deserved this," "You make me do this," and "It is your fault" are examples of irrational thinking.

It is also common for abusers to be aware of and prepare for what the victim may say or do, that is, to role-play the situation in their own minds even before the confrontation occurs. This is a self-fulfilling prophecy. (A self-fulfilling prophecy occurs when one has a thought or plan and acts in ways to make it come true, setting the situation up, as well as attempting to control the other person in following the role one has chosen for them.) This allows the abuser to plan and be aware of his or her future actions. When the confrontation does take place, the abuser's self-fulfilling prophecy occurs.

A common example involves a situation where the victim spends time with a friend of the opposite sex. The abuser may believe that the significant other is unfaithful and has been having sexual relations with the friend. The abuser begins to imagine the two of them together and quickly develops a self-talk which supports this delusion. (A delusion is a belief that is not true and not based in reality, but is held strongly despite evidence to the contrary.) Anything the victim tells the abuser is discounted as a lie, which only serves to strengthen the abuser's delusional thinking. Before confronting the victim, however, the abuser prepares the attack strategies—what to say, how to say it, body language, when to raise the voice, and so on. The abuser may also experience "tunnel vision," seeing and hearing only what he or she wants.

Projection may also occur, and when it does it is a key factor involved in justifying the abuse. Whatever the abuser does not like about him- or herself may be transferred onto the significant other—this is projection. For example, an abuser may be angry or ashamed of something he or she has done. Focusing this anger or shame on the victim allows abusers to feel better about him- or herself and allows a venting of emotions. Another example is that the abuser may have been reprimanded at work or simply have had a bad day at work and may project this onto the victim, taking out the abuser's problems on the significant other. (This process is also referred to as *displacement*.)

Abusers justify violence by blaming their victims not only for the abuser's own problems but for the abuse as well. Statements such as "You asked for this," "You deserve this," or "You make do this" are common but totally untrue. Most abusers tend to feel provoked by their victims, which is a form of rationalization. Rationalization is the abuser's belief that he or she was forced to behave abusively, making excuses for the abusive behavior.

Often abusers speak of "buttons" being pushed. I refer to this as the "He/She made me do it" syndrome. Society reinforces this concept of people having buttons that directly cause us to behave in certain manners. It is often thought that violence occurs in response to certain situations or events. The reality, however, is that abuses are planned events. Abuse does not just happen. No one actually loses control; rather, a conscious choice or decision is made to project responsibility onto one's significant other, that is, to blame the victim.

"Buttons" refer to key words, statements, or situations to which we typically respond. For example, when a significant other disappoints an abuser by canceling a date, the abuser may respond by experiencing hurt or disappointment, which he or she may then quickly turn into anger. What the abuser would remember about this situation is that the canceled date resulted in anger, conveniently forgetting about the hurt he or she experienced or the excuse given for breaking the date. Reality disproves the "button" excuse, however, because if an abuser were truly controlled by buttons, then he or she would respond the same way each and every time the same situation occurred and toward whoever "pushed" the "button," not just toward a significant other.

I want to emphasize that the abuser sets the situation up to allow the abuse to occur. All abuse is a planned, chosen reaction. Thoughts and cognitions play a vital role during the escalation phase. The abuser may tell him- or herself that the significant other deserves to be punished. Common irrational beliefs held by abusers include: "I must be loved by everyone," "I must be respected," "Being frustrated (not having my needs met) is terrible," "I am responsible for punishing or teaching a lesson to my significant other," and "I should be in total control of my significant other." If the victim should walk away from the abuser, the abuser would still believe he or she was being provoked.

Emotional

Abusers experience several emotions, and during this stage most emotions are labeled together as anger. This occurs as a result of not knowing how to appropriately identify and express emotions.

During the escalation stage, abusers may experience anger, frustration, confusion, resentment, guilt, shame, and fear, to name a few emotions. Regardless of which emotions are experienced, it is uncommon for the abuser to correctly identify the emotions being felt. The abuser is confused as to which emotion is occurring, what the actual problem is, and how to resolve the situation. We can all relate to such behavior, because we have all gotten angry at one time or another.

Physical and Behavioral

Physically the abuser's body begins to show signs of increased arousal, also known as the state of *fight or flight* response. Examples include a red face, clenched fists, clenched teeth, squinting eyes, heavy breathing, increased heart rate, and shaking or twitching of the arms, legs, or entire body. Behavioral signs include pacing, shouting, raising one's fist or leg as if to hit or kick, becoming argumentative, drinking or drug use, staring the victim down, and physically cornering the victim.

Red Flag Words and Phrases

Certain words and phrases can act as emotionally charged put-downs. Examples include names that highlight emotional sore spots, such as vulgar names, ethnic slurs, and nicknames that a person particularly dislikes. Phrases that may be red flags include "You're a terrible parent," "You're a bad lover," and others.

At times the phrases may hold some truth, such as when an abuser comments about something that has happened to the victim, but when the intent is to put the other person down, they become powerful reminders of painful reality. Abusers tend to overreact to red flag words and phrases and often will use them to justify their decision to begin the escalation stage.

It is so important to understand that dating abuse and violence does not "just happen" that I will repeat this concept throughout this book. During the escalation stage, there is a buildup of tension involving all five of the cue areas. When anyone experiences tension, he or she seeks ways in which to release this tension. In everyday life, this may include healthy outlets such as treating oneself to a special dinner, a movie, a vacation, or exercise. But when healthy outlets are not easily accessible, not known, or—most commonly—simply not chosen, tension continues to build up until violence may seem the only relief possible. The concept of a volcano is helpful to illustrate the effects of stored tension. When enough tension or energy is ignored, a violent eruption can be expected. The same holds true with emotional tension.

The Victim's Experience

Eventually, the victim feels trapped, helpless, and fearful of the impending abuse. He or she may take responsibility for the abuse, which results in the victim experiencing guilt and shame. Believing that abuse is coming as a result of having seen the abusive pattern of behavior before, the victim may provoke the abuser to get it over with or, in order to avoid the abuse, the victim may attempt to appease the abuser. Most often it does no good. The victim may attempt to do whatever their significant other demands, such as performing unwanted sexual acts, confessing to the abuser or others that the victim is actually to blame, and so on. The result is degradation, fear, and shame.

The victim may attempt to prepare him- or herself for the impending abuse by developing defensive self-talk. For example, the victim may begin telling him- or herself that the abuse is deserved and may make statements such as "If I'd only be less selfish," "He/She wouldn't abuse me if he/she didn't love me," or "I deserve this." The victim may also prepare for the impending abuse by disassociation and by assuming a defensive posture to protect his or her body. *Disassociation* refers to the state of temporarily leaving reality at the time the abuse occurs. It is as if the victim is observing someone else being abused, as if the person is a bystander to his or her own victimization.

During red flag situations, the victim may attempt to "walk on eggshells" in an attempt to avoid fueling the abuser's escalation energy. To do this the victim may avoid certain topics, accept blame for the abuser's actions, or even attempt to leave the situation to avoid being injured. Communication becomes one-sided; the abuser speaks to and for the victim. Again, the abuser hears only what he or she wants to hear and twists the truth to fit the abuser's own twisted sense of reality, which again is part of a self-fulfilling prophecy.

Threats are made, and fear increases. Threatening to leave the abuser or to terminate the relationship usually only serves to increase the intensity of the abuse. It is best to leave the abuser and the relationship *without* giving warning.

During the escalation and explosion stages, abusers welcome any information, threats, or statements that challenge them because these become the justification for further escalation. Abusers will utilize anything they can to avoid taking responsibility for their own actions. It is important to remember that regardless of the actions of the victim, the abuser is always 100% responsible for his or her own behavior and nothing the victim does will lessen the chance of violence happening once the abuser's mind is set.

At times, abuse may be avoided if the victim gives in to the abuser. But this is a catch-22 situation: if the victim gives in, the abuser's delusional thinking is strengthened; but by not giving in, further psychological, physical, and sexual harm may occur in the future. It becomes a matter of survival, and any decision made results in the victim losing. Even if physical or sexual abuse may be avoided, emotional and psychological abuse occurs.

If the victim does give in to the demands of the abuser, the physical and sexual abuse may still occur, although with less severity and intensity than if the victim refuses to give in. Throughout this process, the abuser is 100% responsible for his or her actions, and again, the abuser makes a conscious decision to abuse the victim and therefore is telling the victim loud and clear, "*I do not respect you, and I do not love you.*"

At this point, the victim physically prepares for the abuse and attempts to cover and protect body parts and possessions from harm. The victim may begin to tremble, become hypervigilant of the abuser and of the environment (places to get help or hide). Victims may experience stomach cramps, headaches, neck aches, lumps in their throats, and sweating. In this crisis situation the victim attempts to survive the abuse in any way possible.

The Explosion Stage

Tim tells Bob that Bob is worthless and pushes him against the wall. Bob attempts to get away, but Tim punches him in the stomach. Tim has given himself permission to physically harm Bob.

Betty throws a book at William's picture hanging on the wall, breaking it. William is confused about what is going on with Betty. Betty yells at him and accuses him of wanting to end the relationship. She grabs him by the arm and slaps him across the face. She then storms out of the house, leaving William hurt, injured, confused, and afraid.

Both of these examples could happen to anyone, male or female. In both stories, the abuser vents anger inappropriately, causing the victim to experience harm and fear and damaging the relationship to a potentially irreparable degree.

When the threshold of tension has been reached and the abuser believes that enough justification is present, the next stage occurs: the explosion stage. This stage involves the actual psychological, physical, and/or sexual abuse. This stage is present when the major release of tension occurs, as if a volcano has finally achieved enough pressure to erupt. It is during this stage when the victim's safety is in dire jeopardy. Objects may be thrown and broken. Physical violence may occur and may include pushing, slapping, punching, and using a weapon or object against a significant other. Sexual abuse may also occur, which includes forcing unwanted sexual acts on the victim.

For those who are experiencing abuse for the first few occasions, the explosion stage may only include emotional or psychological abuse. This means that the abuser is at the beginning of the abuse continuum.

The major myth involved in the explosion state is that the violence is uncontrolled, that the abuser has no control once the threshold of tension is crossed. *But the reality is that the abuser is in total control, the abuse is not an uncontrolled act, and the abuser is able to stop at anytime.* However, the abuser may genuinely believe that he or she is actually out of control, despite all the planning that went into the abusive act.

Abusers typically believe that their significant others deserve and need the abuse, as if they are disciplining a child—although with much more force and violence. The abuser thrives on the adrenaline rush that occurs during violence. The more force the abuser uses, the more adrenaline is released and the more the abuser feels in control, powerful, and excited as the victim is forced into complete submission.

During the explosion stage the victim experiences fear and injury and feels degraded, often believing that he or she is responsible for being abused. A sad but common thought passing through victims' minds is "What did I do to deserve this?" The correct answer is "nothing." The abuser planned how, when, and where the abuse would occur, and the victim's efforts to prevent or stop the abuse were futile.

◆　◆　◆

The Honeymoon Stage

The honeymoon stage involves the process of making up after an abusive episode. Apologies may be exchanged and the abuser may even promise never to abuse or hurt the victim again. Gifts may be given, extra-pleasant behavior may occur. Calm and communication may return, but never to the same degree as before the abuse occurred.

In his or her mind the abuser believes that he or she taught the victim a lesson and believes that the victim supported the abuse by not reporting it to anyone, as well as by remaining in the relationship. By remaining in the relationship, the victim also reinforces his or her own role as victim because the message given is that abuse is okay and that the victim somehow deserved to be abused. The victim may feel relieved that the present abuse is over and may begin to feel hopeful that the abuse will never happen again. However, most victims have seen this pattern of abuse before and have heard many broken promises. Still, those who remain in the situation feel thankful the abuse has ended, if only temporarily. The abuser may also experience guilt and shame, but he or she may be unsure of how to cope with and express these emotions.

Steve and Mary are abuser and victim. They have known each other for several years and have been dating for about six months. Mary was originally seen by a therapist for depression, and upon further evaluation her therapist recognized that she was being abused. Mary said that her depression was worse after she and Steve had an argument.

Steve reluctantly came in to see me, making it clear that Mary was the problem and that he was the victim of having to tolerate her mood swings. Steve became angry with me when I asked if he had a difficult time dealing with his anger. I explained that his anger problem had nothing to do with Mary and that he needed to learn about the cause of his anger. Steve gradually opened up and said that when he was stressed and things do not go the way he planned, he became tense and easily annoyed and looked for something to justify venting his anger on her.

We began to discuss the escalation stage. He identified his cues as muscle twitching, neck tightening and aching, narrowing his eyes to focus on Mary, yelling and calling her names, and clenching his teeth and fists. Mary added that when issues of commitment or sex came up, he began to distance himself emotionally from her and even to avoid her at times. Steve's escalation stage usually lasted for about two weeks.

Steve's explosion stage involved putting Mary down by calling her a "slut" and a "bitch," bringing up the fact that she had been abused when she was a child, blaming and labeling her, and effectively devaluing her sense of worth. Sometimes Steve would push Mary against the wall, slam and punch doors, and had even slapped her on occasion. Mary recalls being pushed on the bed and being forced to have sex with him.

After such an episode the honeymoon stage lasted only for a day or two before the next escalation stage began. Steve would bring her flowers, say nice things, tell her he loved her, promise never to hurt her again, and swear that he did not understand why he lost control of himself. Mary would be relieved that this round of abuse was over; but she had seen the cycle before, and her sense of helplessness resulted in a growing depression.

The factors most responsible for victims like Mary remaining in abusive relationships are fear and hope (see Appendix V). Most abusers have a warm, tender side, as well as the hostile, violent side, as did the Jekyll-and-Hyde character. Nearly everyone except the victim sees only the good side of the abuser, which also serves to support the victim in believing that the good, healthy side of the abuser will outweigh the evil, dangerous side. But despite hope, violence occurs again because abuse involves a cycle that feeds itself.

Over time, the abuse cycle escalates in frequency, duration, and severity. As the Escalation of Abuse diagram portrays (see Figure 3), the escalation stage becomes significantly shorter, requiring less and less time to reach the explosion stage. The explosion stage increases in the severity of violence and becomes longer in duration.

The type of force or violence used also changes over time, becoming increasingly severe, as the Continuum of Force diagram illustrates (see Figure 4). The chart shows that there are two types of force, psychological and physical. The types of abuse that occur most often with psychological force are emotional, psychological, and sexual abuse. Most abusers begin by using psychological force against their significant others.

Psychological force is coercion, and there are two types of coercion: psychological strategies and threats. *Psychological strategies* are used to maintain power and control over the victim by using manipulation. There are seven common strategies used against the victim: intimidation, threats, emotional blackmail, game playing, pressuring, boundary violations, and lying (see Figure 4).

Intimidation

Peter asks Emily, "What's wrong with you? Everybody else is doing it. You got me turned on, so now you've got to finish." Peter is intimidating Emily to comply with his demands.

Intimidation is the act of causing victims to experience fear and may be used to coerce them into doing or not doing something in order to avoid further harm. The victim feels fear for personal safety and prepares to be harmed.

Threats

Jody threatens Calvin that, if he refused to do as she said, she would spread rumors that he abused her. Jody is placing Calvin in a difficult position, one in which he is likely to lose regardless

Figure 3. The Escalation of Abuse

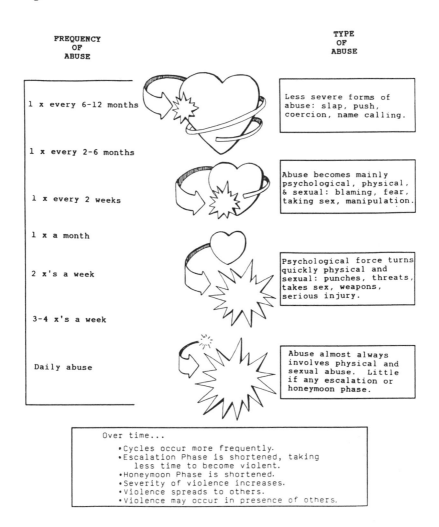

Figure 4. The Continuum of Force

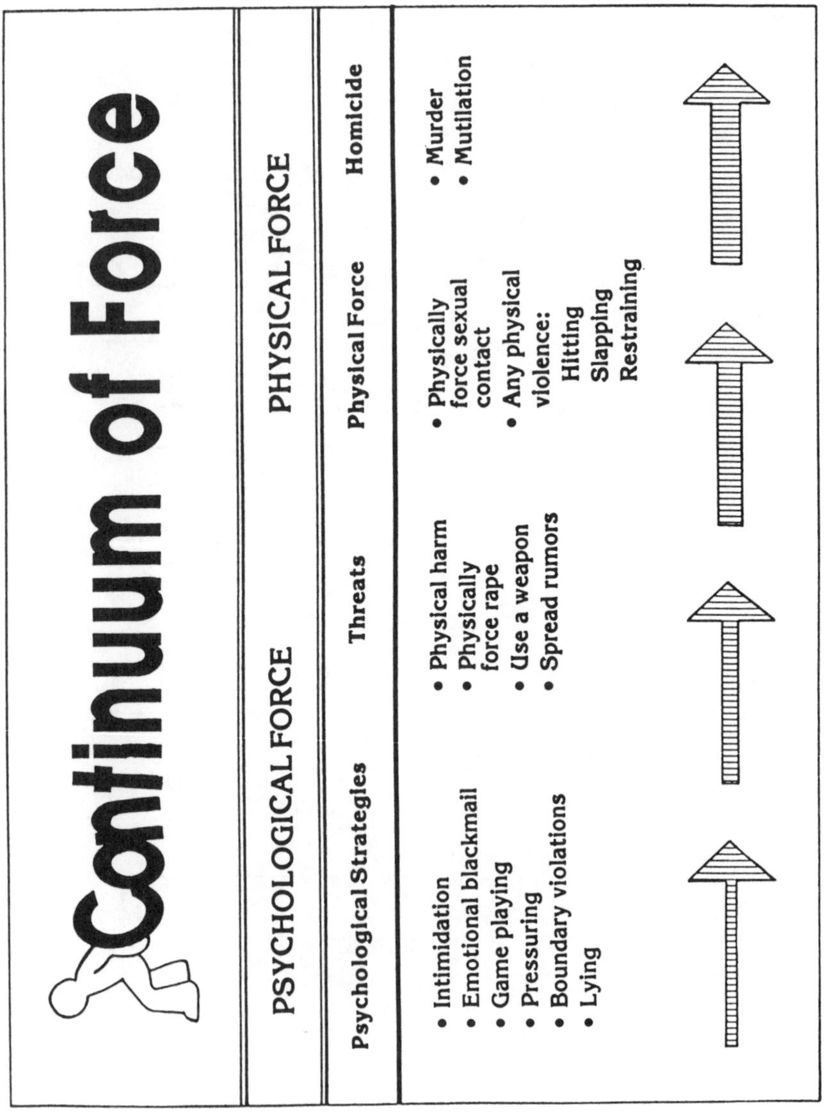

Continuum of Force

PSYCHOLOGICAL FORCE		PHYSICAL FORCE	
Psychological Strategies	Threats	Physical Force	Homicide

• Intimidation
• Emotional blackmail
• Game playing
• Pressuring
• Boundary violations
• Lying
	• Physical harm
	• Physically force rape
	• Use a weapon
	• Spread rumors
		• Physically force sexual contact
		• Any physical violence:
		  Hitting
		  Slapping
		  Restraining
			• Murder
			• Mutilation

of his choice. He will either give in to something he does not want to do or be harmed by rumors that can be extremely damaging.

Threats are used to warn victims of further harm and abuse if they refuse to meet the demands made of them. The abuser may threaten to spread rumors, use a weapon to harm the victim, and may even threaten to further physically and sexually abuse the victim. The victim experiences an increased intensity of fear, while the abuser experiences an increased adrenaline rush, as well as increased feelings of power and control.

Emotional Blackmail

Gene tells Gail, "If you love me, prove it. I've been dating you so long, you owe me sex . . . and a new watch. I've spent so much money on you, you're indebted to me." Gail experiences guilt, powerlessness, and a sense of obligation.

Emotional blackmail refers to using love and other emotions as weapons; for example, threatening to leave the relationship or have an affair, or demanding that the victim do or not do something as a way to prove love and faithfulness. The victim becomes confused, begins to question whether he or she is giving enough to the abuser or relationship, and experiences a sense of obligation to do what the abuser demands.

Game Playing

Dean plays mind games with Becky when he wants her to do something against her will. He tells her, "If you don't have sex with me, I'll find someone who will and then call you tomorrow." Dean also tells her that if she will wash his car, iron his clothes, and clean his house, he will take her to dinner and be "really nice." Becky is confused and experiences guilt as well as a sense of obligation toward Dean. Dean is controlling Becky.

Game playing occurs when the abuser tricks the victim into giving in to demands. Mind games are part of game playing and are intended to make the victim feel crazy and confused.

Pressuring

Sara pressures Mike to take her to an upcoming concert instead of his awards ceremony. She continues to beg, saying, "Oh, come on . . . please." Mike feels the pressure from Sara and feels he needs to take care of Sara's demands.

Pressuring refers to the nagging and begging used to gain the cooperation of the victim. The victim is not given the option to refuse the abuser without feeling guilty, selfish, and abnormal.

Boundary Violations

Elaine makes comments about Jerry's body when he is within hearing range. She tells him, "I think you have a sexy body and would love to touch you all over." Jerry feels uncomfortable with Elaine's comments and tells her to stop, that he does not want to be talked to like a sex object.

Victor makes sexual gestures toward Renee when they are alone. He grabs his crotch, blows kisses, and moves close to her, sometimes rubbing against her. She has told him to stop and that she was not interested in him. He ignores her requests.

Boundary violations occur when the personal space of the victim is not respected. The abuser may begin to physically touch the victim's body, remove clothes, or prevent them from leaving. Boundary violations can occur at work, school, clubs, bars, church—anywhere. The legal term for boundary violations is *sexual harassment,* and it is subject to prosecution under today's laws.

◆　◆　◆

Lying

Cindy promised Nathan when he took her to a concert that they would go steady. The day after the concert, she told him, "Thanks, it was fun, but I only wanted to go to the concert."

Lying refers to the promises the abuser makes in order to make the victim do something but that the abuser does not keep.

The seven psychological strategies are ways in which abusers control and abuse victims. Over time, however, these strategies do not result in the same feelings of power and control, and the adrenaline rush that results also diminishes over time, becoming less intense and less satisfying. As a result, the abuser progressively begins to use more severe types of force, moving along the abuse continuum to the second type of coercion (psychological force), which are threats. Once again, however, the intensity of the adrenaline rush and feelings of power and control diminish and no longer satisfy the abuser. When this happens, the abuser moves further along the continuum of force and begins to use physical force, which includes both physical and sexual abuse.

Some abusers are not satisfied with the results of physical force, so they progress to the end of the continuum, which may include torturing, mutilating, or murdering their victims.

All abusers use increasingly severe forms of abuse and violence over time. However, although not all abusers progress to the extreme of homicide, most if not all abusers will eventually progress to using threats and physical force. Just as athletes need to increase the amount of effort and time invested in their workout to achieve the same feelings of power and control, as well as an increased adrenaline rush, so too the abuser increases the amount, frequency, and severity of the abusive behavior.

The honeymoon stage becomes shorter over time, with less of a make-up period. Eventually the three-stage cycle becomes a two-stage occurrence, a continuous escalated state leading to the explosion stage. The cycle begins to repeat itself more frequently.

For example, early on abuse may have happened once every three months, then once every month, then weekly, and then even daily. But no matter how often it occurs or how severe the type of violence, it is still violence, violence is abuse, and abuse is wrong, against the law, and in no way associated with love.

Steve and Mary, the couple whose story I told earlier, continued in therapy. Steve identified that he had used the following types of force on Mary. He physically and sexually abused her when he pushed her, held her down on the bed, and raped her. He used intimidation when he raised his voice, called her names, put her down, punched or slammed the door, by making focused eye contact with her, and by the fact that the abuse occurred in the past and that it could occur again at any time with little or no warning. The fear of what he had done to Mary would forever haunt both of them. He threatened Mary by raising his fist or leg (to kick), by any quick movement during his abuse, and by directly warning her that he was going to abuse her. He constantly crossed her boundaries every time he hurt her.

Steve lied to Mary every time he promised never to abuse her again. He pressured her into having sex, and he used sex as a weapon, a tool to vent his anger. Emotionally Steve blackmailed Mary into staying in the relationship, giving her the message that if she did not do as he said, he would hurt or leave her. Steve pressured Mary into doing things she did not want to do, such as having sex, making him dinner, and so on. Some of the abuse involved several types of force, such as physical force, emotional blackmail ("you owe me"), intimidation, threats, and game playing.

Whether they remained in their relationship or ended it, as a result of the violence between them both Steve and Mary would need to relearn how to trust and deal with issues of intimacy, sexuality, communication, and problem solving. Before they would be able to maintain a healthy relationship with anyone, they would both have to change. Both would have to live with the memory of this abusive relationship for the rest of their lives.

The Effects of Abuse

Most of the effects of dating violence cannot be seen or physically detected, but they can be heard when speaking with victims of abuse. Dating violence affects the victim, the abuser, the dating relationship, and society.

The Victim

Victims of abuse often lose the most precious part of lives, ownership of their own lives and bodies. Losing the power to control one's own body is a frightening experience. Instead of focusing energy on the good things in life, a person focuses all his or her energy on surviving day-to-day battles.

The victim also loses self-esteem, trust for others, feelings of safety and security, and his or her own sense of development. Deep confusion occurs; it is difficult to cope with loving one's significant other on the one hand, yet hating and fearing that same person on the other. Victims experience shame about being victimized, guilt for not being able to stop the violence, and feelings of worthlessness believing something must be wrong with them or they would not be abused.

Victims also experience great uncertainty about the future, hopelessness, depression, and suicidal thoughts or attempts. They may quit their job or school, use or abuse alcohol or drugs to cope, or become submissive or aggressive in an attempt to survive. Increased medical problems may arise due to physical injury, as well as stress-related illnesses. Often the victim is forced to stop associating with friends and even family members in order to hide the abuse, and this results in a decreased social network.

Over time a victim may even believe that he or she is crazy.

This occurs as a result of others denying the experiences of the victim, especially if others reinforce the myth that the victim deserves to be abused. The victim often loses any sense of pride, control, and dignity as the abuse continues.

The Abuser

Abusers may hate themselves for behaving abusively but deny they have the power to change. They may insist that somehow they are the real victims. Abusers thrive on controlling their significant others and may actually encourage their victims to take the blame for the abuse and to feel crazy. Many abusers were victims themselves at one time. They are aware of the humiliation, hurt, fear, and pain involved in being victimized but somehow believe they are justified in abusing their significant other. It is as if they choose to validate their own experiences as victims by victimizing others.

The longer the abuse continues, the stronger the abuser's irrational or distorted thinking becomes. Physical complaints, headaches, ulcers, and stomach problems may begin to appear due to the abuser's inability to deal with stress. Emotionally the abuser begins to experience increasing jealousy, anger, and impatience toward others, and others may become aware of the abuser's problem. Also, the abuser may begin to abuse the significant other in public and may abuse others as he or she begins to feel invincible, justified, and immune from prosecution. Increased alcohol or drug use and abuse also commonly occurs, which the abuser may use to justify violent behavior. Abusers may utilize suicide threats or attempts and may even threaten to kill their victims as a means to maintain control. The severity of the abuse always increases over time.

The Relationship

Abuse wreaks havoc on relationships. The abuser holds

most of the power and relies on violence and abuse to maintain this power. Abuse becomes an expected, accepted occurrence.

Communication becomes one-sided, with the victim not being heard or respected. The relationship becomes much more rigid as the abuser becomes increasingly disturbed and paranoid. The couple becomes isolated from others. At this point the relationship is dead, and the abuser is not capable of loving the significant other. Again, this is due to the abuser believing that their significant other is an object, a possession for the abuser to do with as he or she pleases. *Remember that love has no place for objectification, lust, or greed.*

If the abuser and victim marry each other, the abuse will still continue and will become more severe and intense as time goes by. In the past marriage was often thought to somehow "cure" abusive tendencies, but this is a myth. Marriage requires much more commitment, teamwork, and trust then any dating relationship. Inherently, marriage results in much more stress than a dating relationship.

It is difficult ending any abusive relationship, but ending an abusive marriage is far more complex. There is property to divide, spousal support, child support, severe emotional stress, extended family division (grandparents' visitation, aunts and uncles), and so on. The bottom line is this: If abuse is occurring in the dating relationship, then abuse will continue to occur in the marriage with much more force and severity.

The couple may spend less time in public and more time alone as a way to prevent the person being victimized from seeking support or help. The relationship cannot grow and therefore begins to stagnate. Stagnation leads to a spiral decline in the quality of the relationship until it finally dies.

Society

Abusive dating relationships adversely affect society in

several ways. First, if abuse is allowed to occur—that is, if abuse is not recognized by the community as a serious problem—then abuse becomes an accepted standard of behavior. Second, if relationship violence is condoned, then it will not be long before any type of violence toward others is more common and, worse yet, accepted. In this case the quality and integrity of society would become more barbaric, with violence and abuse so out of hand that there would be little or no protection available. Third, children learn more from their family relations and observing other people in their lives than in any other way. If children observe violence being tolerated and even condoned, the cycle will pass from generation to generation. As a result, laws against abuse will become weaker than they already are. A time might come when the law and the community in general will simply not get involved with relationship violence issues.

CHAPTER FOUR

How Abuse Is Learned

People learn to behave abusively in many ways, and of these there are three primary problems that most abusers experience: low frustration tolerance, power and control issues, and jealousy.

Low Frustration Tolerance

Low Frustration Tolerance (LFT) occurs when people believe that they are unable to tolerate or effectively cope with discomfort and frustration. As a result of this belief, a person would attempt to avoid any situation that might result in discomfort or frustration—for example, not having a person's needs or demands met when requested, being challenged by others, and even the possibility of not being in total control of oneself, others, and situations. When a person genuinely believes that he or she is unable to cope with events, the person develops beliefs that support the problem (this is a self-fulfilling prophecy).

Such beliefs in return influence certain emotions and behaviors to occur, such as avoiding situations in which one may not have the power to be in control, or either not making needs and requests known or aggressively making needs and demands known. The quickest method to do this is to become abusive. The stronger the beliefs that a person has LFT, the more this person believes him- or herself to be actually out of control, and the more abusive the person may become.

When a person with LFT is faced with conflict, he or she will usually seek power and control.

Power and Control Issues

Power and control issues also serve as a primary underlying problem for every abuser. The belief that the abuser needs to be in total control of him- or herself, others, and the world is clearly evident when examining the behavior of an abuser and when reviewing the Abuse Chart (Figure 1). Power refers to the desire to have control or influence on others, such as what they do and who they see. Control is power in action and is the actual state of exerting power over others, that is, actually making someone do what one wants. Power and control are beliefs that people hold and are maintained by strong but irrational core beliefs. It would be unrealistic and impossible to always be in total control of anyone, ourselves included, or in total control of any situation. But most abusers believe that they should be and hold strongly to this belief.

When an abuser exerts power and control over a victim, moving through the escalation stage and into the explosion stage, adrenaline is released. The adrenaline may produce a pleasant feeling. It may result in a high, a heightened sense of excitement, such as when riding on a roller coaster. This adrenaline rush is no different than the rush a person experiences when he or she runs or works out. Unfortunately, the abuser may see the adrenaline rush as a reward for abusing a significant other.

Some people become addicted to the adrenaline high and are referred to as adrenaline junkies. When this occurs, they will engage in any behavior that results in the release of adrenaline. Risky behavior, violence, and impulsive behavior often provide the quickest and most potent adrenaline rush.

Jealousy

Jealousy is often present when abuse occurs. Jealousy refers to a belief that a person owns something and attempts to protect the object from being taken away from them. The primary problem jealousy presents is that *jealousy always refers to an object, not a person*. When an abuser acts jealous, it is because the abuser truly believes that the significant other is an object, a possession to be owned. The abuser objectifies the victim. Jealousy always leads to irrational, unhealthy behaviors and is a form of psychological abuse. (Jealousy will be discussed in more detail in Chapter 6.)

These are the three primary underlying reasons that people choose to abuse their significant others. However there are other factors that may influence a person's choice. It is important to remember that although any of these factors may significantly impact a person's life, they do not cause abuse to occur.

Violence in the Home

Violence within the home ranks as the most important factor in the acceptance of violence in relationships. When children observe their parents arguing and abusing each other, the message the children hear is that abuse is the appropriate manner for the expression of anger or frustration. When children are actually physically or sexually abused, the lesson is reinforced. Statistics indicate that approximately 80 to 90 percent of abusers and victims have observed family members being abused or were themselves victims of abuse as children.

Society

Socially, violence is reinforced daily. On television and in the movies violence is portrayed as acceptable and, at times, the only sensible reaction to stress, frustration, and anger. Most often the abusers get away with their crimes, thereby strengthening the social acceptance of violence. On the football and baseball fields, hockey and ice rinks, boxing and wrestling rings, violence appears condoned whether provoked or not. For example, it would be rare for an athlete to be arrested for assaulting another player during a game. Also, much too often when there is a rape scene in a movie, the victim somehow seems to change his or her mind and enjoy the rape, thereby relabeling rape as an act of passion.

To refute these lessons is a difficult job, but it is imperative that we do so. In real life no one wants, enjoys, or deserves being emotionally, physically, or sexually abused—ever.

Laws also reinforce the idea of abuse and violence as acceptable, first by the lack of laws pertaining to relationship violence, and second by the level of difficulty often experienced by the victim in prosecuting the abuser. The fact that most athletes and abusers get off with minimal plea-bargained sentences speaks to the social acceptance of violence. Even when arrested, many athletes and abusers spend little time in jail, regardless of the severity or nature of their offenses.

Cultural Factors

The "macho role" and "machismo" foster the belief that men, by nature, are violent and that it is acceptable for men to abuse and/or rape their significant others. This role encourages men to behave in a controlling, aggressive manner. Many men believe that they are expected to be in constant total control of their significant others and that the use of violence to keep them in line is expected. Even today there exist communities where the attitude toward men who commit physical and sexual assault is that "boys will be boys" and prosecuting the abuser is next to impossible.

Difficulty with Emotions

Difficulty expressing and identifying emotions can also lead to aggression. Men typically have a difficult time with the emotions of jealously, isolation, anger, love, caring, and fear. *Jealousy*, which will be discussed later in Chapter 6, is an emotion that always leads to abuse and is always toxic to a relationship. When jealousy is present, love is absent because the two are opposites.

Some men have a difficult time being isolated, even for a short period of time. *Isolation* usually includes feelings of insecurity, inadequacy, and abandonment. Men sometimes believe that they must be taken care of by their significant others and that they can not take care of themselves.

Anger, to many men, is equated with provocation, a lack of ownership, and a lack of control. To be angry is to be justified in abusing others. Anger is one of the catch-all emotions. What this means is that anger is often identified as the emotion being experienced when in fact another emotion, usually one more difficult to cope with is occurring. When a man who has this belief system directs anger toward a significant other, chances are good that he is really angry at himself and is displacing and projecting his anger onto the significant other, blaming the person for his own miserable feeling.

Fear is an emotion that may also result in abuse, and a person can experience fear of almost anything. For example, an individual may have a fear of losing his or her significant other; of not being a good significant other, parent, or friend; of being alone; of what others may think about him or her; and so on. Fear makes people aware of the fragility of reality, that nothing is ever guaranteed as permanent, and that at anytime those we love may choose not to be around us any longer.

The healthy result of fear that most people ignore is that it encourages us to treat others with respect. Fear can help us to remember that our significant other is making a conscious choice to share his or her life with us and that relationships are always changing. Therefore, relationships demand that we change over time and not fear the uncertainty that occurs in any healthy relationship.

Mental Illness

Mental illness may increase the chance of abuse occurring because it may affect the abuser's pattern of thinking and reality testing. Examples include paranoia and narcissism, which distort the thinking processes. This accounts for only 15 to 20 percent of abusers. Although mental illness affects the judgment process, individuals suffering from mental illness often use their psychological disorders as an excuse to continue to behave inappropriately.

If a mental disorder results in an increased chance of violence occurring, and the individual refuses to follow the recommended treatment (therapy, support groups, or medication), then this individual may need to be institutionalized in a supervised living arrangement or, in the worst case, prison for their own safety as well as the public's.

Drug and Alcohol Abuse

Chemical dependency and abuse (the addiction, misuse, or abuse of a drug or alcohol) often is blamed as the cause of abuse.

It is easy to understand this assumption, because approximately 75 percent of abusers are under the influence or alcohol or drugs before, during, or after the abuse occurs. However, there is no evidence that alcohol or drugs cause abuse. Certainly when an individual is under the influence of drugs or alcohol, he or she may act differently than when sober (taking more risks, increasing aggression by giving him- or herself permission to behave in these ways). Alcohol and drug use does result in an altered state of consciousness, but the person remains in control of his or her behavior. Behaving abusively is always a choice.

For example, alcohol *decreases* a person's motivation, making a person tired by depressing the central nervous system. Any sense of increased energy is a misperception, a distorted interpretation of the effects of alcohol. Therefore, to become aggressive while drunk requires an extra amount of energy and a predetermination (decision and plan) to be violent.

When alcohol or drug use causes violent behavior, it is usually due to damage to the brain resulting from long-term chemical use or mixing prescription drugs with other drugs or alcohol. The difference here is that when such an individual becomes violent, he or she will attack whoever is around, not just his or her significant other. They would not be able to selectively choose their victim. When a person is using alcohol or drugs and becomes violent only toward a significant other, it is his or her *choice* to abuse that person. Alcohol and drugs do not *cause* the abuser to abuse.

When the abuser suffers from blackouts, he or she may forget some of the details concerning a particular period of time or event. This forgetfulness is assumed to somehow allow the abuser to take less responsibility for his or her actions. A common defense goes something like, "If I can't remember how I behaved, then I did not mean to do it and I must not have been in control." This excuse occurs in spite of the details provided by the victim about how the abuser glided through what appeared to be pre-planned escalation and explosion stages.

Forgetting what happened is no excuse for an abuser's behavior, and in no way does it relieve the person from receiving consequences for his or her actions. The abuser *was* in control and was keenly aware of how he or she behaved. The proof of this is that the abuser was able to respond to the victim's behavior and comments and was able to adjust his or her behavior accordingly. The same is true if a person is a drunk driver and is able to make it home. The individual is aware that he or she was intoxicated (or at least impaired) and had to adjust his or her driving to avoid collisions, make turns, stop at lights, and so on. My point is that even drunk drivers have enough awareness at the time to react to others and to make decisions about how to act. Blackouts do not excuse abusive incidents, and when pushed hard enough, the abuser often experiences an amazing recall of events.

Rigid Beliefs

Rigid beliefs are common factors which lead to abuse. When people cannot bend or change such beliefs, they may experience an increase in tension, which in turn increases the likelihood of choosing abusive behavior.

Rigidity leads to seeing things in black or white, right or wrong, either/or terms. It is as though there is an absolute right or wrong with no need for exceptions or "gray" areas. Often abusers state that their significant others cornered them into being abusive and that the victim deserved and even asked to be abused. Rigidity leads to an increased sense of self-righteousness, of believing one somehow possesses the ability to judge others, as well as to be responsible for punishing those who do not listen.

Religious Beliefs

Fanaticism can also result in abuse. When a person who is overly strict is rigidly obsessive about a religion—for instance, one is which the man is considered to be the boss or "head" of the household—abuse is more easily disguised as discipline. Many abusers who are religious fanatics use scripture as a means to justify abusing their significant other or children. The abuser misinterprets scriptural passages and uses them out of context. But the Bible in no way justifies abuse; in fact, it offers several passages against abuse, violence, child abuse, drunkenness, and jealousy.

Despite such misguided beliefs, people are always in control of their emotions and behaviors and always have several options for each situation they find themselves in. Even when the above factors are present, it is still a choice to behave abusively.

One couple I counseled whose case had elements of religious fanaticism was Peter and Lori. Peter and Lori had been dating for over a year. Peter's parents followed a small cult-like religion and raised Peter to obsessively follow their beliefs. One of these beliefs was that the man held the power in a relationship and that the woman was to be submissive to his needs and not achieve outside the home. This presented a problem for Lori, who wanted to finish college and was even considering graduate school. Peter flatly informed her that she could not continue to attend college and that she should not make plans to work unless the job was menial and part time.

Peter further told her that she could not spend any time alone with male friends and that he expected her at home with dinner on the table when he arrived. If she was late getting home he would blow up. He frequently intimidated and threatened her and believed that it was alright to punish her for acting in ways that, according to him, only sinners and sluts acted. He was jealous of any male friends she had, although Lori had never been unfaithful to him. Lori was expected not to argue with Peter, even when Peter was wrong and unfair.

Hearing this, Lori became irate. Who was this man to order her around, to tell her which job to work at, or to determine her educational limits? She told him that he could not control her life and that if he continued to treat her abusively, she would leave him. Peter's parents became involved, scolding Lori for talking back to their son. Later, Lori attempted to discuss her concerns with Peter. She explained that her family values were different and that she expected and demanded to be treated with respect.

This was the last straw for Peter. He cursed her, grabbed her by the hair, slapped and punched her, and threw her down on the floor, where she lay bleeding. He threatened that if she ever refused his wishes again, talked back to him, embarrassed him in front of his parents, or attempted to maintain friends of whom he did not approve, she was "really going to get it." Lori got the message loud and clear: if she refused to be Peter's puppet and victim, she was going to experience further harm. She left that night and called the police. Peter was arrested for domestic abuse and making terroristic threats.

Lori began to get the support she needed at a support group for abused women. In our sessions together, I explained to her that no one deserves to be abused, ever. It took a while for her to believe me, but she finally did. Peter fought the therapy process. He argued that Lori was to blame, that she was a sinner, and that men are supposed to be in charge of any relationship. Peter stated that it was Lori's fault that he had begun to abuse alcohol and that when he became drunk he could not control himself. When I told Peter that alcohol did not cause him to do anything, he became frustrated and quit therapy.

From the beginning Lori had recognized that something was not right in her relationship with Peter, and after the first incident of physical abuse she left. This probably saved her life.

Lori's family had open communication, encouraged the members to achieve whatever goal they were able to, and supported each other. It was not a perfect family, just an average family. Peter's family held rigid beliefs, giving no one room for personal growth. Peter became paranoid as his attempts to have total control over Lori failed. His abuse of alcohol increased. The alcohol helped to medicate his loneliness, and the only security he felt from others was when he was in total control of them. This relationship ended.

Although violence is often learned by observing others, particularly parents who are abusers, this is not an excuse for new violent behavior in adulthood. Unfortunately, thousands of children live in abusive and violent homes. However, most go on to become conscientious adults.

CHAPTER FIVE

Emotions and Abuse

Emotions are the feelings that give quality to life, adding intensity, color, and meaning to our experiences. Emotions in and of themselves are neutral, neither good nor bad, healthy nor unhealthy. However, the behavior we choose in response to emotions *can* be healthy or unhealthy. Certain emotions such as respect, caring, and love are more likely to encourage us to make healthy behavior choices, while other emotions such as hate, jealousy, and anger may encourage us to behave in unhealthy ways.

Many people believe that emotions simply happen and that we are powerless to decide which emotions will be experienced. However, emotions do not just happen, but rather are the result of certain beliefs we hold; that is, our beliefs determine which emotions we experience. Beliefs provide a guide that each person uses to interpret and evaluate experiences. For example, if we hold a belief that it is important to treat others with respect, then we are more likely to experience the emotions of caring, respect, and love. If we hold a belief that it is important to be in control at all times, or that our needs must be met at any cost, then we are more likely to experience the emotions of frustration, jealousy, and anger.

Not only do our beliefs help determine which emotions we

will experience, but we can adjust the intensity of the emotions ourselves. This process is accomplished by using the "emotional thermostat," which can increase or decrease the feelings. For example, when an emotion occurs, we can decide what intensity the emotion will be and adjust the thermostat accordingly. If we place an emotion on a continuum, it will be easier to see our options. For example, *love* could occupy the middle ground between *like* and *idolize*:

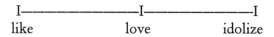

I————————I————————I
like   love   idolize

Angry could occupy the middle ground between *annoyed* and *hostile*:

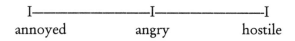

I————————I————————I
annoyed   angry   hostile

If we put every emotion on a continuum before we act on it, then we can see the choices we have. If we experience anger and want to act violently, then we would adjust the thermostat from *angry* to *hostile*. Remember that all emotions are neutral when they occur, and we adjust the emotions by increasing or decreasing the intensity of the emotion or by choosing to leave the intensity as is.

Learning to correctly identify or label which emotions we experience can be difficult. No one is ever 100% accurate in identifying and correctly labeling all of their emotions, and this is not a goal anyone should strive for. However, it is important to be able to correctly identify an emotion that is at least similar to the one we are experiencing, because it is extremely difficult to change our behavior if we are not able to appropriately identify which emotion is occurring. Often when we behave inappropriately it is the result of an emotion we find to be too painful, frightening, or confusing.

Basically the choice when an emotion occurs is to acknowledge and appropriately express the emotion, or to deny, ignore, and bury it. It is not always advantageous to express emotions as they occur. In times of crisis, such as when experiencing any type of victimization or loss, it is common and often necessary to deny or repress some emotions in order to cope with the crisis at hand, giving attention only to those emotions of immediate concern.

For example, when Dave is abusing Sara by pushing and cursing her, Sara can not safely identify and cope with all of the emotions she is experiencing. Sara has to prioritize which emotions need immediate attention. Emotions such as fear of immediate safety, of being killed or seriously injured, need to take priority. Also during times of crisis we may not think as effectively as when we are not in a crisis situation, so all the options available to us may not be clearly seen.

Regardless of whether we deal with the emotions at the time they occur or at a later time, eventually we will have to deal with them. Emotions will find some way to be expressed, either directly or indirectly. Coping with emotions in a healthy way involves three steps. Most of the time people complete all three without necessarily thinking about them.

The first step is *identifying* the emotion. Far too often emotions are labeled as either good or bad, happy or sad. We do this because these emotions are commonly accepted by society and involve less risk to express than other emotions. Yet we must correctly identify which emotion is occurring before we can begin to adequately and effectively cope with it. For example, if we are experiencing frustration but label it as anger, we cheat ourselves of the true emotion of frustration.

The second step is *acknowledging and accepting* the emotion, even though it may be uncomfortable, embarrassing, or frightening to experience. This allows us to openly experience the true emotion that is occurring. If we do not accomplish this step we deny ourselves the color and meaning that emotions add to our experience, as well as the right to proudly and honestly accept the emotions that occur.

Step three is *appropriately expressing* the emotion. If we are experiencing the emotion of hurt but display anger, two things may occur. First, others may react with defensiveness and hostility, when what we need is support. Second, by behaving angry instead of hurt we do not allow ourselves the expression of hurt, therefore limiting and narrowing the emotions we allow ourselves to experience. To accomplish this step, we must have completed steps one and two and must be willing to take the risk of expressing our true emotions. Learning to follow these three steps takes time, practice, and much patience.

Ask yourself, "Which emotion does it make sense to be expressing in this situation?" Then name the emotion, acknowledge and accept it, and decide how to express the emotion. Correctly identifying which emotion is being experienced and which emotion is being expressed involves skill and insight. These three steps present one effective way to deal with difficult emotions.

It is also helpful to use the cue areas (discussed in Chapter 3) to help identify which emotions are being experienced. What are the cues we are experiencing? If we are tense, have clenched fists and a tight jaw, an upset stomach, and a red face, then we are probably experiencing anger or frustration. These are some of the symptoms of anger and frustration, and not all of these symptoms have to be present. If we feel queasy, have a lump in our throat, shaky arms, legs, or hands, are teary, and are avoidant of others, we may be experiencing fear.

At times we may find it easier to ignore, bury, or disassociate from certain emotions. However, when emotions are stuffed or buried, we do more than cheat ourselves of the emotion. We also create deeper problems, such as increased stress and problems with concentration. Moreover, the emotions may be expressed directly or indirectly, which results in the building up of raw emotion, such as with a volcano. The more we stuff and bury, the more sensitive we become to others, sometimes becoming increasingly volatile and sometimes withdrawn. When enough emotion has been stuffed into the volcano (our gut), the result can be an intense explosion of raw emotion, just as a volcano erupts. As a result the emotion released intensifies. For example, if the original emotion that was buried was frustration, the emotion can become intensified and explode as anger or hostility.

Despite the intensity of the emotion being expressed, however, we remain in control of our behavior. Some people choose an easy way out, allowing raw, uncensored emotion to be expressed. This usually takes an extreme form of behavior. Such extremes are usually overly passive or aggressive. The more we stuff, the stronger the explosion of raw emotion, the more severe the behavior we choose to do. Someone suffering from depression may turn to suicide; someone suffering from an eating disorder may turn to binge-purging or starvation. In these instances the person turns the violence inward and attacks him- or herself. But when the behavior is directed toward others (projection), abusers often vent their aggression towards their significant others. This is dating and domestic violence.

Again the concept of choice applies here, because the abuser consciously makes a decision to hurt either him- or herself or the significant other. When the volcano containing the repressed and buried emotions finally erupts, it does *not* cause a person to behave in any specific manner; the person continues to have the power to choose how to deal with the problem, either by attempting to work it out or by using violence.

When it becomes clear that we are mislabeling an emotion, we have the power to relabel it. There are three areas of focus when attempting to change an emotion. The first is to focus on which emotion we are *experiencing*, the second is to focus on which emotion we are *expressing*, and the third area is to focus on the *beliefs we hold.*

Deciding which emotion we are experiencing appears to be an easy task. Unfortunately, many people mislabel the emotion, leaving the person unsure of which emotion they are actually experiencing. Mislabeling may occur for several reasons, which may include:

• Not understanding or being able to differentiate which emotions are being experienced, which occurs when a person is confused and unclear of what emotions are. The most helpful way to overcome this problem is to use a list of emotions.

• Several emotions may be occurring at the same time, which can cloud or mask the emotions being experienced. When we experience a flood of emotions, it is important to ask ourselves, "Which emotions are most important in this situation?" If we are having difficulty doing this, ask, "Which emotions should be occurring given this situation?"

• As a defense mechanism, our mind may attempt to protect us from an emotion which may be too painful or frightening to experience at this time.

Attempting to identify which emotions we are experiencing can be accomplished several ways. First, we can look at our behaviors. What are we doing? How are we behaving? Are we storming around and swearing, or are we calmly talking with someone? Second, we can ask for feedback from others. Someone may tell us that we appear hostile, angry, calm, or sad. We may have difficulty observing our own behaviors primarily because we may *think* we are behaving calmly when we are actually behaving hostilely. Others can more accurately perceive and identify our behaviors, and we can benefit from their observations. Third, once we have identified which behaviors are being expressed, then we can examine the beliefs we hold which support the emotions and behaviors we choose.

When attempting to change an emotion, it is imperative that the focus be placed on the beliefs we hold verses focusing on the emotions directly. That is, we should focus on the process by which our emotions are chosen. Therefore, changing our beliefs may change the emotions we experience.

Fear

Fear is a complex emotion that we experience as a result of feeling threatened. Fear can be healthy or unhealthy, depending on whether it is based in reality and whether it is significantly interfering with our lives. Fear may include uncertainty about a relationship, a person or ourselves. Common fears include the fear of being harmed or killed, of losing our significant others, of a relationship ending, of being a bad person or significant other, of looking bad or losing face, of not realizing our dreams (attaining a degree, a vacation, a marriage, maintaining a job), of letting ourselves down, of being alone, and of consequences resulting from our behaviors. Fear represents our awareness that we may be in danger, that things change, and that nothing is forever. The healthy quality of fear is that when it is based in reality, it keeps us aware of the need to treat others with respect and to respect ourselves. Fear also allows us to accept and expect change and growth. Most important, however, is that fear tells us when we are in danger. When fear occurs, trust it—it is usually very accurate.

Anger

Anger often occurs as a result of mislabeling. Anger is the displeasure we experience with something or someone. Although anger appears to be the emotion that leads to abuse, it often represent only a small path on the long road to abuse. Anger is often used to justify abuse—the idea being that somehow the abuser is not responsible for his or her actions—because society supports the beliefs that anger is the result of provocation and that provocation is enough justification for violence to occur. However, the reality is that anger is a choice; it does not simply occur as a result of provocation. And anger does not cause abuse; abuse is a chosen behavior.

Frustration

Frustration represents our awareness of unfulfilled needs or demands. Frustration may result when things do not happen when we want them to, when our needs are not met to our satisfaction, when we are not able to clearly or effectively communicate our needs or wants, and when we lose patience. Frustration can be affected by Low Frustration Tolerance (LFT).

Hope

Hope refers to the belief that things, situations, and people can change for the better. Society and religion encourage people to have hope, and they foster the belief that people will change for the better if given enough time. Everyone is *capable* of changing their beliefs and behaviors, but this does not mean that certain people will ever do so. Again, change involves work and risk, and most people will only attempt change when their current behavior is painful, uncomfortable, or unfullfilling. Victims may give their abusers the ultimatum that the abuser either stop behaving abusively or the victim will leave. But ultimatums rarely result in changed beliefs and behaviors, and the hope victims hold on to often results in more severe abuse.

Anyone can stop abusing their significant other for a short time without help. What helps them succeed is the knowledge that after a certain amount of time has passed, they may return to the old problem behavior. However, the fact that people can and do stop their abusive behaviors, even for a short amount of time, offers proof that the abuser is always in control of his or her behavior.

Love

Love is the intense feeling of pleasure a person experiences for those people for whom the person cares deeply. Love involves intimacy and spirituality as well as trust and respect, not only for others but for oneself as well. Love is the warm, comfortable sensation experienced when one is with one's significant other, or just thinking of him or her. Love is knowing how, when, and what to say, and when to compromise with one's significant other. Abuse and love are opposites; when abuse is occurring, love is absent.

Isolation

Isolation is a real or perceived state of aloneness. When isolation is experienced, it is often due to an abuser preventing a victim from having a support system or of the abuser's having been overly dependent on a significant other. Isolation results when an individual is unable to see that he or she has choices and therefore does not ask for help and support when he or she needs it most. Abusers do everything in their power to create the feeling of isolation in their significant others, and because of it victims begin to isolate themselves from others in order to avoid further abuse or embarrassment.

Abusers may also isolate themselves by avoiding friends and family and by staying home with their victims as often as possible. The abuser attempts to prevent anyone finding out about the abuse and attempts to prevent the victim from leaving the relationship and getting help. Thus the victim is without others, without support, and alone.

Power

Power refers to the amount of control that abusers and victims experience. Victims experience powerlessness because abusers do whatever they want. Victims are not allowed to express concern or make requests. Abusers experience power over victims by dictating what the victims will do, say, and even who the victims can see.

Jealousy

Jealousy refers to the fear of losing something a person owns or possesses. Jealousy does not involve trust or respect, and therefore cannot involve love. It is the fear that something owned will be taken away. Jealousy is a form of psychological abuse because the abuser objectifies the victim.

Confusion

Confusion refers to the uncertainty we experience about something or someone. It usually results when people are unclear about what a person wants, feels, or is attempting to communicate. Confusion may encourage victims to feel crazy or to blame themselves for abuse.

Abusers and victims experience each of these same emotions:

	Abuser	**Victim**
Fear	• of losing significant other • of losing face/reputation • of losing control	• of harm • of losing dignity • of losing significant other • of losing security
Anger	• misdirected at victim • self-fulfilling prophecy • (sometimes) at self	• at abuser • at self for not leaving • may blame self for abuse
Frustration	• of unfulfilled demands, real or imagined	• of failed attempts to leave relationship
Hope	• of demands being met when first made • that victim will remain in relationship	• that abuser will change • that abuse will end
Love	• of self • of power	• of abuser/significant other
Isolation	• from anyone who would not tolerate abuse	• from anyone who would expose/end abuse
Power	• exerts power • thrives on domination • feeling of ownership	• lacks power • loses sense of ownership of body and life
Jealousy	• lack of trust and respect • objectifies victim	• of others' relationships
Confusion	• of how to communicate effectively • of what he or she really wants • of why victim does not meet demands	• of why he or she is being abused • of how to get help • of his or her rights • of his or her own sanity

The emotions that occur as a result of dating violence affect both the abuser and the victim. While abusers thrive on certain emotions to help them move through the cycle of abuse, victims may attempt to avoid certain emotions as a way to survive the abusive situations.

CHAPTER SIX

Redefining Jealousy

Jealousy is an emotion supported by a rather complex pattern of thoughts. Semantics often create confusion about jealousy, which is generally unhealthy, as opposed to concern, which is generally healthy.

Concern can be viewed as the active part of love. Concern refers to caring for another person. It is the energy we choose to invest in our significant others that focuses on their well-being, putting their needs before our own. Concern is based in reality. We may experience concern over our significant other's health, job, or abusive behaviors. Concern does not involve controlling behaviors.

A relationship is an ongoing process involving commitment, flexibility, respect, and honesty. A relationship based on love and concern is an ongoing process, a process that evolves, changes, and is challenged over time. People involved in a healthy relationship understand that commitment—the fact that someone decided to share his or her life—is a privilege. They welcome this challenge and are not threatened by the uncertainty it brings.

Envy refers to wanting something that another person has. Envy differs from jealousy in that envy is based on reality. One may choose to cope with envy in healthy or unhealthy ways.

Healthy ways to cope with envy would involve working for a desired object or earning the respect and cooperation of a person from whom one would like something. Envy becomes unhealthy when an individual allows it to brew. Then it can lead to anger, resentment, and jealousy. Over time the individual may become bitter toward the person who has what he or she wants.

Jealousy and anger are the emotions that abusers most often admit to experiencing and most often use to justify violence. Jealousy refers to the state of suspecting rivalry or infidelity, with most energy invested in guarding a possession. Jealousy implies ownership of something. In general, emotions are neutral, neither healthy or unhealthy; it is how we choose to behave as a result of an important emotion that can be unhealthy. Jealousy is the exception to the rule.

When jealousy is expressed toward a significant other, it always results in abusive behavior, and jealousy is always unhealthy. This is due to the mistaken beliefs a person holds which support jealousy. Therefore, when a partner tells us that we cannot do something or see certain people, power is being exerted; they are controlling us as if we were an object or possession they own. When the security of ownership is threatened, a person may respond by becoming angry and fearful about the potential loss. However, most abusers do not correctly identify and label the fear, only the anger, which fuels the jealousy.

Jealousy involves the fear of losing something, of having something taken away. As I have said before, *a prerequisite to losing something is owning it, and no person can ever own another human being!* Jealousy also implies a perceived power imbalance, and this is the abuser's mistaken belief that he or she owns the significant other.

For example, Paul attempts to prevent Valerie from spending time with others, especially her male friends. Paul automatically assumes that she is engaging in sexual intimacies with her friends simply by the fact that she spends time with them. In order to prevent her from maintaining any source of support, as well as to eliminate any competition for her, Paul does everything in his power to prevent or sabotage any relationship Valerie establishes. He twists the truth to fit his delusion that Valerie is having an affair. However, the delusion is Paul's belief that he owns Valerie.

Jealousy always results in inappropriate and abusive behavior. Jealousy deteriorates relationships, and if a person views his partner as a possession, the jealous person is not respecting the partner. For instance, if the potential abuser were experiencing concern instead of jealousy about the significant other leaving, then the abuser would be more likely to feel fortunate to be able to share a life together. People are more likely to be concerned about their partners' well-being than being focused only on their own.

It is important to compare jealousy and concern so that the differences can be seen and appreciated. The primary difference is that jealousy is the belief that a person owns the significant other whereas concern is expressing the reality that the significant other may choose to end the relationship, being aware that life offers few guarantees.

Jealousy	Concern
Based on irrational thoughts.	Based on reality; uses rational thoughts.
Misperception of data, of other's intentions. Involves cognitive distortions.	Thoughts and beliefs based on accurate data and interpreted by beliefs based in reality.
Domination: one is up, one is down.	Equal power; decision making is shared.
Fears losing significant other, usually based on misperception.	Fears but accepts that significant other may want to end relationship.

◆　◆　◆

Figure 5. The cycle of jealousy is perpetuated by not taking
responsibility for one's actions, by the belief that one owns
one's partner, and by believing one is "out of control."

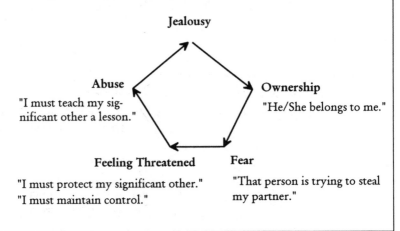

The process of how people develop jealousy is illustrated in Figure 5. A belief can be inferred from self-talk (what one tells oneself), from statements the person makes, and by the person's behavior. The first stage in this process is the idea of ownership. This involves the belief that an individual owns his or her significant other, that the other person belongs exclusively to the potential abuser. Statements such as "He/She is mine", and "He/She belongs to me" may occur with jealousy, demonstrating the beliefs a person holds concerning their significant other being viewed as an object they own.

The second stage is fear. This may include the fear of losing the significant other (either by the person choosing to leave or by someone stealing them away) and fear of the relationship ending. Common examples of self-talk and statements that may occur here include "He/She is looking to meet someone else so he/she can leave me" and "That person is trying to take my significant other from me."

The third stage is feeling threatened. During this stage there is an attempt to maintain power and control over the partner due to a perceived threat of loss. It may be perceived that someone else is interested in and is going to attempt to steal the significant other or that the significant other is looking for somebody else. The basic thought going on at this time is to maintain and protect the possession, the significant other. This may include restricting where the significant other goes and who he or she sees.

Examples of self-talk and statements that may occur here include "I must protect my significant other," "He/She is naive and needs to be protected from being taken advantage of by someone else," "I need to use whatever it takes, including force and physical violence if necessary, to keep him/her," "He/She asked for and deserves to have me keep them in line," "He/She must be punished and taught a lesson if he/she tries to leave me," and "I need to show him/her how much I care."

In such cases the abuser confuses object love with person love. At this point the abuser is so fearful of losing the significant other that he or she believes that abuse is the only way to prove how much the abuser loves the victim and the only way to keep the victim. In this stage the abuser develops a plan of action for the abuse. The abuser plans what to say, when and how to say it, and considers how to act. Plans can involve hours, days, or even months worth of planning and scheming, or may take only a few seconds. The stage is then set for the abuse to occur.

The next stage is the actual abuse. The abuser may use verbal, psychological, physical, and/or sexual abuse at this point in an attempt to maintain control over the significant other. The abuser has talked him- or herself into feeling justified in using violence to maintain control over the significant other. Thoughts such as "He/She asked for this," "He/She misbehaved and must be taught a lesson," and "I wouldn't do this if I did not love him/her" may occur. From this stage the process begins all over again.

The abuser may make comments such as "See what you made me do," "I'm sorry, but I lost control," and "I love you so much that I don't want to lose you." These are all signs indicative of abuse involving jealousy. The jealousy cycle is perpetuated by irrational thinking and will continue to occur because it is a negative feedback loop, that is, it continues to feed on itself without accepting new data. This is how jealousy occurs. Every emotion involves a similar process of developing supporting beliefs before the emotion occurs. However, most emotions are based on rational, not distorted, thinking.

Developing a specific belief system involves and requires hard work. The first step is to name what one wants to believe. For example, in order to "own" a significant other, a person must believe that the significant other is an object to be owned and then believe the abuser actually owns the person, as well as viewing the person as an extension of the self.

Step two is the development of support for the belief. When support comes from reality, it is often sound. When support for a belief is not based on reality, however, it is referred to as a *delusion*. Delusions make sense to the person holding them, but not to others. Delusions are strongly held beliefs that persist despite evidence that proves them wrong.

We control behaviors by our thought process, which includes beliefs. We can also control our emotions by our belief system. I refer to this as the "emotional thermostat" mentioned in Chapter 5. The emotional thermostat is the process of adjusting the intensity of a feeling. Before turning the thermostat up or down, however, a person must first place the feeling on a continuum (see page 64). For example, at one end of the anger continuum we may be upset, while at the extreme end we may be hostile. Where the person is on that continuum is based on that individual's belief system. It is the person who chooses to turn the thermostat up or down, placing him or her at one end of the continuum or maintaining equilibrium somewhere in the middle.

No one controls you, and no one can provoke you into action. It is always your choice how you respond.

An advantage of focusing on the important role jealousy plays in dating violence is understanding that jealousy does not cause abusive behavior; rather, an abuser chooses to use jealousy as a justification for committing abuse. Emphasis can then be placed on the abuser. Most people have difficulty dealing effectively with jealousy, but that does not justify using jealousy as an excuse. Jealousy is not healthy and always results in inappropriate and abusive behaviors.

Jealousy also deteriorates relationships. If a person views a significant other as a possession then he or she does not respect the significant other, but rather objectifies the significant other. Jealousy is in no way associated with love. If a person believes that he or she is fortunate to share life with a significant other, he or she is less likely to take the person for granted and more likely to view the significant other as a person rather than an object. Jealousy may be the label for an emotion, but when it is present irrational thinking and mistaken beliefs are also present. Therefore, if a person is experiencing the emotion of jealousy, then he or she is also having irrational thoughts that support jealousy. However, that person still remains in control of his or her behavior.

The story of one woman whom I counseled illustrates how jealousy affects the victim. Pat often became upset when Leslie spent time with her friends. Leslie had had these friends for many years and spent time with them at least twice per week, usually when Pat was working or out with his friends. Pat yelled at Leslie when she had been with her friends and called her a whore, a slut, and a bitch. He told her that he knew her male friends all wanted to have sex with her and that none of her female friends liked him.

Leslie offered to bring him with her when she went out with her friends, but he usually refused. When he did go along, he was overpossessive of her, not allowing any of her male friends near her. He even threatened one of her male friends whom she wanted to hug. Things worsened when they were alone. When she refused to have sex with Pat, he accused her of having affairs. No matter how she explained to him that her friends accepted that she was dating him and would never ask for sex from her, he ignored her. He called her a liar and denigrated her until she doubted her own sanity.

Pat told Leslie, "You're mine. No one will want you if you see your male friends again; I'll make sure of that." Leslie was frightened and confused; she had not been unfaithful to Pat. She tolerated his abusiveness and even stopped spending time with her male friends, but nothing satisfied Pat. Not only did he not believe that Leslie was not seeing her male friends anymore, but he also demanded that she not spend time with her female friends.

Leslie was expected either to be with Pat or to wait at home until he called or came over. He made it clear that she had better listen and do what he wanted or he would end the relationship. Most people involved in such an abusive relationship would say, "Forget this, I'm leaving. I do not deserve to be abused." However, Pat had stolen Leslie's self-esteem. She gave him her time, her money, and sex. She believed that to lose the relationship would be to lose the only sense of worth, value, and belonging she knew.

Eventually Pat began to physically abuse Leslie. He grabbed her by the arm, forced her to listen to him, and humiliated her when alone and in public. He even began to rape her, forcing her to have sex with him upon demand, and to put her down for not sexually pleasing him. He blamed her, objectified and sexualized her, and became paranoid and obsessed with her. Leslie was in danger and unable to see any source of help that could save her. Her depression grew, as did her suicidal thoughts. On her fifth try at suicide, she almost succeeded. It was in the emergency room that help finally reached Leslie.

The doctor who resuscitated her was concerned about Leslie's emotional health and sent for the chaplain and the social worker. They told Leslie she was a victim of dating violence, explaining that she had worth as a person and that she did not deserve to be abused. After leaving the hospital, Leslie became connected with a support group for victims of abuse, and she began therapy with me as well. In therapy she learned that she had much to offer herself and others, and with support from both her old and new friends, she succeeded in putting her life together—without Pat.

CHAPTER SEVEN

The Role of Cognitions

"I really hit the ceiling when you talk about my ex-wife," John, a short, paunchy forty-year-old, said to his new wife, Linda. Often we hear people complain that something or someone caused them to experience a certain emotion or caused them to behave in a particular manner. The implication is that situations and other people control our feelings and behaviors. According to such a theory we cannot choose what to feel or how to react to others.

Albert Ellis, the founder of Rational Emotive Therapy (RET), strongly disagrees that we are helpless to the forces of others. He believes that we control our emotions and behaviors and that others cannot control us. Ellis developed a working model to illustrate how cognitions really work. This model is referred to as the ABCs. The intricate details of the ABCs of RET are complex, but understanding the basic principles should be of help in defining irrational thoughts.

"A" refers to the activating event or situation one is responding to or being affected by. This may be a confrontation with someone or something not turning out the way one desired.

"B" refers to our belief system, which is the most important component in controlling our emotions and behaviors. We use our belief system to evaluate and give meaning to events based on the values and morals that make up our belief system. Beliefs are our guide to interpreting data and events. Beliefs affect how we choose to adjust the emotional thermostat.

"C" refers to the emotions we experience following the activating situation, or "A." Based on the emotional response, we choose how we will behave. It is common for people to believe that they move from "A" to "C." They believe that the event caused their emotional or behavioral response to occur. The most important and often overlooked part of this model is "B."

Most, if not all, abusers believe that "A" (situation) causes "C" (emotion), which in turn dictates which behaviors occur. This belief leads to the irrational conclusion that the abuse occurs simply as a result of an emotion, and that they are unable to control their behavior (see Figure 6).

Holding this belief, abusers begin to feel that their abusive behavior is out of their control, that it simply occurs as a result of emotions. If this were true, every time the abuser experienced the same situation it would result in the same emotion, and the abuser would behave in exactly the same manner each and every time. For instance, John is an abuser who is prone to violent behavior. If we accept this theory, every time John experienced anger he would become violent toward whomever was accessible. In

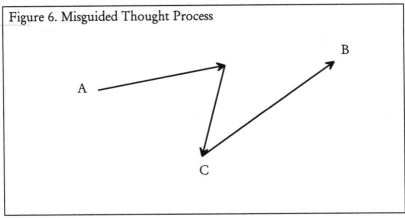

Figure 6. Misguided Thought Process

various situations John would become violent toward his boss, other family members, friends, co-workers, and strangers. Yet this isn't true either for John or other abusers. Most abusers only attack their significant others. This offers one significant proof that abuse is a controlled, planned act in which the abuser chooses to engage.

What was not taken into account here in our theory of John's behavior is the belief system ("B"). It is our belief system that allows us to analyze a situation and react with a particular emotional and behavioral response. This is how it works: A situation happens ("A"), our belief system ("B") evaluates and analyzes the data, and then, based on our beliefs, an emotion ("C") occurs. When this happens, we choose the degree of emotion that will be experienced by adjusting our emotional thermostat. Adjusting the thermostat to the desired intensity, we choose a behavior to express that degree of emotion (see Figure 7).

If there are certain situations that we continually have difficulty dealing with, we may choose to avoid these situations if possible. However, we may not always be able to do so. There are two types of "As": those we can change and those we cannot. When certain situations create problems with our beliefs, or when something or someone challenges or threatens our beliefs,

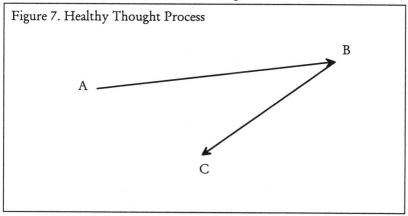

Figure 7. Healthy Thought Process

we can choose to avoid these situations or people or modify or change our belief system that pertains to these specific situations, thereby offering ourselves different choices to which we may respond.

For example, Jane hates visiting her stepmother, who is overly critical of Jane. Jane tries to avoid going to her father and stepmother's house. Like Jane, if visiting a certain person creates problems for us, by challenging our beliefs, then we could choose not to be around that person. However, some situations we cannot control. Examples for Jane included her father's serious illness. She could have avoided going to her father's house in this situation, but the thought that her father might die and she wouldn't see him was enough to make her visit. Like Jane, we cannot change or avoid all unpleasant situations. Therefore, we may modify or change our belief system. Changing or modifying our beliefs may allow us to cope with unpleasant as well as pleasant situations in a healthy manner (see Figure 8).

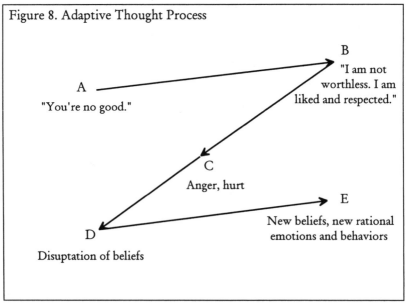

Figure 8. Adaptive Thought Process

A
"You're no good."

B
"I am not worthless. I am liked and respected."

C
Anger, hurt

E
New beliefs, new rational emotions and behaviors

D
Disuptation of beliefs

There are two kinds of beliefs: rational and irrational. Rational beliefs are true and result in moderate emotions and behaviors. They help us attain our goals and are not rigidly right or wrong, black or white. When we experience stress in relation to a situation and our beliefs are rational, the stress level would probably range between the 30% and 70% level, a range well within normal limits.

```
——————————I————————————————I——————————
0%         30%        50%        70%        100%
```

Irrational beliefs are not true and result in extreme ranges of emotions. They are based on erroneous and irrational data. They prevent us from attaining our goals and are often commands or absolute in nature. According to Walen, DiGiuseppe, and Wessler, irrational beliefs fall into four categories.

The first category contains *"awfulizing"* statements. Examples include "It is awful when you do not meet my needs" and "It is awful when things do not go the way I want them to." This is also referred to as *catastrophizing*. We can only believe that something bad will happen, and we blow things out of proportion.

The second category contains "should," "ought," and "must" statements. These are absolute statements that dictate that a specific course of action needs to occur, and there is no room for other choices. This is black-and-white, either/or thinking. There is no room for any middle ground or "gray" area, and as a result a person must choose between two extremes.

The third category includes *need statements*. Abusers often confuse desires with true needs, resulting in erroneous beliefs about what one's needs truly are. The reality is that we need very little in life. Food, water, shelter, and clothing may be real needs we have, but companionship and relationships are also needs. However, we do not need to have sex whenever we become sexually aroused, and reality has proven that if our requests are not met immediately we will still survive.

The fourth and last category includes beliefs concerning human worth. Often abusers and victims doubt their self-worth or doubt the worth of their significant others. Statements such as "You're no good because . . . ," "I must be a failure because . . .," and "I must not count because . . ." are the type of statements abusers and victims may feel and say. Abuse often clouds reality. When worth is conditional, dependent on how one behaves, that in itself is abusive and irrational. All people are worthwhile regardless of what they choose to do or not to do.

There are three characteristics that apply to irrational beliefs, and some irrational beliefs may include more than one characteristic. They are (1) a philosophy of self-denigration (putting oneself down), (2) Low Frustration Tolerance, and (3) blaming and condemning others. Irrational beliefs are maintained by self-indoctrination. This includes focusing on the irrational belief and may even reach the extreme of obsessing on the belief, as well as telling ourselves repeatedly that these irrational beliefs are true.

Cognitive Distortions

Cognitive distortions refer to faulty thinking. Most people at some time in their lives use distortions in thinking in order to see and hear what they want to. These distortions also serve to vindicate certain behaviors, especially when these behaviors are abusive. Cognitive distortions include the following.

• *Polarized thinking* is seeing things as all or nothing, black or white, with no middle ground. This is also referred to as absolutist thinking. Either things are going great or they are terrible. For example, our significant other either loves us totally or does not care for us at all.

• *Overgeneralization* is making mountains out of mole hills. It involves taking whatever is happening in a certain situation and generalizing to all situations. For example, if our significant other hurts or disappoints us, we believe that all people we trust and care about will also hurt and disappoint us.

• *Thought screening* is seeing and hearing only what we want to and disregarding the rest. For example, if our significant other had a problem keeping the plans for a date and explained that he or she would be late or unable to show up, all we focus on is how he or she affected us; we disregard the reasons for the changed plans, even though the explanation might be legitimate. All we seem to hear is that the person canceled the date, and that our wants were not met. It is as though a filter screened out all information that we did not want to hear.

• *Discounting* is similar to thought screening. Anything positive that happens is minimized, and we prepare for an imagined or expected negative reaction. For example, if our significant other gives us a gift, we assume that something must be wrong, that they must have cheated on us or want to end the relationship. If they give us a hug, we may tell them that it meant nothing. Discounting is similar to *minimization.*

• *Snap judgments* involve making assumptions and decisions without considering the facts or without taking time to think about how to react. An example would be seeing our significant other with another man or woman and assuming they are having an affair. The reality may be that the person was innocently having coffee and talking, but we come to the decision that the person is having an affair without asking for clarification. Snap judgments are not based in reality, and we had no evidence to back them up.

• *Exaggeration* is blowing things out of proportion, giving more meaning to something than is warranted. For example, if a partner gives us a gift and asks us to go to a dance or a party, we might assume that this means she or he wants a deeper relationship, wants to have a sexual relationship, or wants to marry, when in fact the person may simply enjoy spending time with us without wanting to deepen the relationship. We gave too much meaning to their behavior. Another example would be to become irate with a partner when he or she tells us they have to cancel plans. To the person who exaggerates the issue is paramount while in fact it may be insignificant.

• *Minimization* involves underestimating something or someone, not giving credit when credit is due, and expecting too much and never being satisfied with what a person gives. Let us say we receive a gift from our significant other and complain that it is only a piece of silver jewelry when we wanted gold; or at a party we cause him or her to feel less important than our friends, the event, or something else. Minimizing can involve never accepting what our significant other offers, as if the person owes us so much more when in fact they are offering a lot. For instance, Joelle expected many expensive gifts at Christmas and only received two or three inexpensive ones; she spent the day pouting. Minimizing the meaning of what a partner says because of high expectations would be another example.

• *Emotional reasoning* involves interpreting a situation based on an emotional reaction or feeling. For example, if we had a good day at work, we might believe that we must be a good person. If we have an argument with someone and are feeling angry and sad, we feel we must be a bad or worthless person. If we are sexually aroused, we may believe that our significant other is also sexually aroused simply because we are. Basically this type of reasoning involves using emotions to decide who a person is and what the person's worth is.

• *Absolute statements*, or imperatives, are unrealistic demands and expectations. They use the words "should," "ought," and "must." They are setups for failure, because they can seldom be met and are often irrational and unfair to impose on anyone to begin with. For example, if we believe that our significant other "should" have sex and she or he refuses, we become angry and feel let down. It may even appear to be a devastating letdown because of our unrealistic demands and beliefs. To believe that "it would be nice if he/she had sex with me" is a healthy replacement for the "should" belief because it allows our partner to say no without feeling as if he or she has caused a major catastrophe.

• *Labeling and mislabeling* involve objectifying ourselves or our significant others. For example, Mary sometimes wanted to be intimate with Ted but did not desire to have intercourse. Ted called her a "tease" when this occurred, thus objectifying Mary. Other examples include racial, religious, or sexual putdowns, all of which take away an individual's identity.

• *Personalization* involves an assumption that things happen because of us or that others are always referring to us. For example, our significant other ends the relationship with us, and we believe that we caused her or him to leave. The reality, however, is that we may have influenced the person to leave, but we did not *make* the individual leave. Another example is hearing two people talking and noticing them looking in our direction several times; we assume they must be talking about us when in fact they were simply looking at the clock behind us.

• *Rationalizations* are excuses used to justify behaviors. Telling ourselves that we have spent so much money and time with a significant other that she or he now owes us sex is one example of rationalization. Another common rationalization is believing we are out of control, which is never the case. Rationalizing basically means giving ourselves permission to do or not to do something and involves finding excuses and reasons that support our decision. However, we always have the power to make a decision. Whether this decision is to back off, to fight, to brutalize, or to rape, it is in our power to decide.

All of the above are types of cognitive distortions. Though abusers often use such thinking to justify or excuse abuse, they are never excuses.

Distorted thinking can damage a relationship as well as our self-esteem. At some times everyone uses cognitive distortions to cope with situations; however, we must pay attention when we use them. If a person's primary method of problem solving is using distorted thinking, then that person is in need of education and therapy to learn healthy problem solving skills.

To demonstrate how cognitive distortions can damage relationships and increase the power of abuse, let us look at one couple: Tom and Jim. When Tom became stressed, he quickly became irritable and frustrated. He had a short fuse and at times seemed to almost beg people to argue with him. Jim recognized Tom's escalation pattern very well, having been involved in a relationship with him for over two years. In a tense mood, Tom would criticize, and when really stressed, he would challenge Jim's love for him.

Tom carefully screened everything Jim said to him. When he found the smallest inconsistency, he blew it up, making it into a major issue. One day Jim had spent the morning with his mother, the afternoon with a friend named Greg, and met several friends in the evening. It was his night away from Tom and Tom's night for bowling. When they got together Tom was livid. "You spent the whole day with Greg," Tom shouted. "You would rather be with Greg than with me." Jim sighed, "On one hand, this is true, because Greg treated me with respect, but I'm really faithful to you."

In my therapy session with Tom and Jim, Tom continued to hear only what he wanted to and discounted much of what Jim said. Jim wanted to resolve his issues and to improve and save the relationship. Tom also wanted to save the relationship, but minimized any responsibility for their problems. It took several sessions before both agreed that their relationship was abusive and that Jim was the victim. Tom reluctantly accepted that the way he treated Jim was verbally and psychologically abusive. Interestingly, Tom stated that his father would often put his mother down and would belittle any accomplishment Jim or his siblings made. His father expected everyone to jump through hoops before getting any sort of acceptance or approval.

Tom was trained badly by his father and chose to continue the cycle of abuse in his own relationships. In our sessions, Tom learned to listen to what was being said, to hear the message before responding. This helped him recognize how he would twist the messages from Jim to fit what he wanted to hear. He was surprised at how good it felt to really listen and hear Jim's messages. Jim learned how to let Tom know when he was not listening by telling Tom to stop and let Jim finish or restate his message.

The relationship between Jim and Tom showed other signs of victim and abuser roles that had to be worked on. Tom also stereotyped men to be provocateurs of abuse, and this came from his father mostly blaming the abuse in their childhood home on Tom. Tom viewed Jim as an argument waiting to happen, somehow always deserving to be put in his place. As our meeting progressed, Tom finally understood that he had learned to be abusive from his father. He felt relieved that he wasn't born an abuser. Most importantly Tom learned that he could change the way he viewed women and men and make a conscious effort to empower Jim instead of taking power away from him.

CHAPTER EIGHT

Relationships and Abuse

We all search for that special someone to share our lives with, someone with whom to share our dreams, successes, and failures. Yet many people have not yet developed and matured as individuals, which is a prerequisite to becoming constructively involved in any relationship.

Relationships serve several purposes, including friendship, advice, companionship, acquaintance, and romance. Some people hold the belief that a single person can fulfill all of a person's needs for affiliation. If we expect our significant other to fulfill the roles of friend, confidant, advisor, and so on, this is a difficult, perhaps impossible, demand to fulfill. To impose it on one person may deeply frustrate that individual.

Other consequences of having these unrealistic expectations may include irritation, arguing, increased distance between partners, and unhealthy communication. Often the result is an unhealthy relationship. The couple ends up further apart, while emotionally clinging to each other at any cost, because to lose each other would result in aloneness and isolation.

Most people do not fully understand what a relationship is, nor do most people truly understand what to expect from others or how to treat others. This chapter is in no way intended to serve as in-depth guide to relationships, but rather as an overview of what a relationship is and what it requires from each person, and to describe and contrast healthy and unhealthy relationships.

The most important aspect of any relationship is that it is a fluid, ever-changing interaction and exchange of affection and energy. No relationship is guaranteed to be permanent. Each person must continually work at maintaining it. A relationship is an intimate, romantic, passionate attachment between two people. A relationship has three identities, and together the three form a triangle. Figure 9 illustrates what a healthy relationship looks like.

A healthy relationship demands that all three identities are separate, and each must be allowed to grow. Not only can a healthy relationship withstand having others involved, but it *demands* the involvement of others.

Each identity should also have clear boundaries. Remember that a relationship is always changing; therefore, each person or identity should be allowed to grow individually and independently, as well as to grow closer together. All identities are equal in a healthy relationship.

Unhealthy relationships are illustrated in Figures 10 and 11. In Figure 10, the relationship consumes each person's identity. Both people give up their dreams, goals, and individuality and

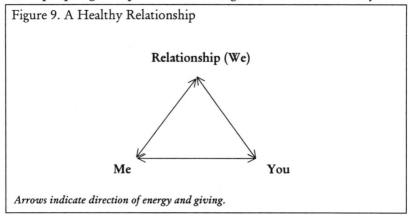

Figure 9. A Healthy Relationship

Relationship (We)

Me   **You**

Arrows indicate direction of energy and giving.

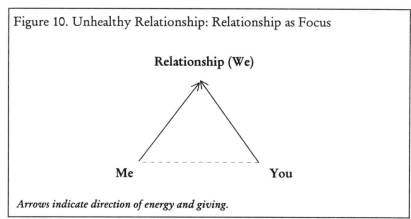

Figure 10. Unhealthy Relationship: Relationship as Focus

Relationship (We)

Me   **You**

Arrows indicate direction of energy and giving.

eventually become consumed by and trapped in the relationship. People who center their lives on the relationship, who do not have a separate identity or support network, are commonly in this type of relationship.

In Figure 11 the relationship centers on the demands and requests of one person. Abusive relationships almost always look like this—a one-up and one-down situation—where the focus of the relationship is on maintaining a tenuous equilibrium, and the only way to do this while maintaining the fragile relationship is to be a victim.

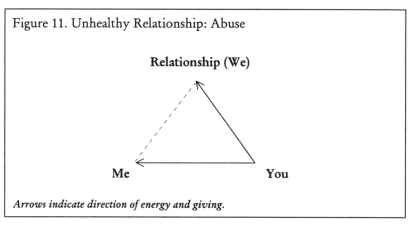

Figure 11. Unhealthy Relationship: Abuse

Relationship (We)

Me   **You**

Arrows indicate direction of energy and giving.

When a relationship is unhealthy, neither person dares to be separated from their significant other for any amount of time out of fear of losing or sacrificing the small amount of self-identity they have managed to hold to. It is as if their individual identities are so fragile that they believe they may disintegrate without the other person. Both people are dependent on the relationship, and neither are likely to do anything that may jeopardize the security of the relationship.

Diane often became frustrated with Amy and blamed her for not listening to her concerns. Diane believed that her communication skills were fine, that she clearly identified what she was feeling, and that she told Amy about them directly when she needed to. Amy thought of ending the relationship, because she felt that Diane *rarely* told her how she felt. Both agreed that they argued too much, but neither agreed on what the arguments were about. Diane admitted that she blew up at Amy but could only identify that she felt angry.

Although Amy's ability to correctly label and appropriately express her emotions was not perfect, she was able to communicate fairly effectively. Diane, however, clearly demonstrated to me that she had difficulty with emotions. Diane clearly stated when she was angry but lacked any awareness of other emotions. When Diane was hurt, she buried the pain. When she was scared of losing the relationship with Amy, she became blaming and angry. It took abut three months before Diane learned enough about emotions to be willing to explore the emotions she experienced.

Diane learned that when her needs were not met, frustration, not anger, should occur. When this happened and she was let down, she learned to label this as frustration or disappointment. Most of all, when she was scared, this often meant that she was having a difficult time becoming more emotionally intimate with Amy. In the past she would become anxious, tense, and angry with Amy, blaming her and even accusing her of cheating on her. This would become abusive when Diane called Amy names, objectifying her.

Now Diane tells Amy when she needs to talk. When she becomes tense and scared, Diane holds Amy's hand and they talk. Diane has learned that only she can control which emotions she experiences, and only she is in control of taking risks with Amy by sharing her true feelings. Diane learned that being honest about her emotions was risky, but it was a risk worth taking.

Abusers believe that their significant others are around to meet any and all of their demands made in exchange for not psychologically, physically, or sexually harming the significant others. Abusers expect their significant others to meet any request or demand made of them or else suffer further harm. Abusers may expect their significant others to:

* Have sex after a date.
* Not see people other than the abusers.
* Drop whatever they are doing to please the abusers.
* Put their goals and dreams aside and focus only on the abusers' demands.

The abuser dominates both the significant other and their relationship. As time passes the abuser will grow ever more domineering and controlling over their victim and nearly always believe that they own their victim. Because of the belief that they own their significant other, abusers tend to view the time with their victims as being "spent" rather than "shared" with them.

Many people choose to settle for "spending" their life rather than "sharing" their lives with someone. There is a major distinction between the two. Spending implies having something and exchanging it for something in return. Love cannot be bought, while food, flowers, gifts, candy, and clothing can be.

When a person spends time with someone it is as though he or she gives something up and exchanges it for something of lesser value. For example, an individual may choose to give up money or loneliness because he or she wants the commodity (significant other/victim) to replace a present situation or to somehow improve it. Nevertheless, the idea of "spending" time with a significant other results in an empty form of intimacy.

Effectively sharing a life with someone involves a non-possessive attitude. By sharing a life with a significant other, a person becomes aware that the relationship may not last forever and that it is important not to take the other person for granted. Sharing implies that both people are giving as well as taking. The power in a sharing relationship is equal, because both people are investing themselves in the relationship. Therefore, sharing is a much healthier attitude and fosters a healthy relationship.

Healthy relationships are a complex process, an ongoing, even exchange between two people. What is exchanged includes trust, time, commitment, intimacy, and caring. These are not things you see, but rather emotions and behaviors symbolic of caring and love. To give these parts of oneself to another person requires a comfort with and knowledge of oneself. To attempt to give them to others without first comfortably giving these to one-self is a form a masochism. Doing so would deprive oneself of dignity and respect. One must first understand, care for, respect, and love oneself before being capable of caring for, respecting, or loving another person.

Eric Fromm, a well known psychoanalyst whose work con-tributed to the development of the existential approach in psychology, illustrates this point extremely well. Fromm believes that human beings are constantly aware of and struggling to over-come feelings of isolation, aloneness, and separateness and that of-ten people choose to enter into a relationship as a way to cope with these feelings. However, it is not possible to overcome these feelings once and for all, and a relationship will not take these feelings away. As a way to cope with these feelings, Fromm de-clares that we should strive for what he calls *relatedness* (some way to relate with others) and for identity (at-oneness, an identity that separates one from others) before entering into a relationship.

Indeed, before a person is capable of loving another person, the individual must first love him- or herself. To do this one must apply the elements of love to oneself. This basically means becoming aware of who you are—that is, your identity—being responsible for, respecting, and knowing yourself. It makes sense that you can never give to others what you have not yet given to yourself. Any attempt to do so results in empty forms of intimacy and, therefore, an unhealthy relationship.

In an attempt to seek relief from the feelings of isolation and separateness, a relationship often seems the quickest route. However, it you do not yet love yourself, then you are not capable of loving another. Fromm identifies four alternatives for meeting one's needs when one has not learned to love oneself. Fromm's first choice is extremely pertinent to our discussion of dating violence.

Fromm refers to it as an *orgiastic state*. An orgiastic state is a temporary state of elation, similar to a state of self-induced trance. An orgiastic state may be the quickest way to gain temporary relief from the feelings of loneliness, isolation, and separateness. According to Fromm, all orgiastic states have three shared characteristics:

1. They are intense, even violent at times;
2. They occur in the total personality;
3. They are transitory and periodical.

Examples of orgiastic states include having sexual orgasm, using drugs and/or alcohol, and violence.

Sex provides a relief from the buildup of anxiety and tension. Sexual intimacy and orgasm can also create a false sense of closeness, belonging, and love. However, the intensity of these sudden feelings and tension release soon lead back to guilt, shame, and an increasing sense of isolation. This is due to the lack of solid spiritual relationship: two strangers who shared intimate acts together, but spiritually are empty because they do not yet love themselves, and did not take the time to build a solid relationship.

The high or quick fix of sexual orgasm is much like that afforded by alcohol and drugs. Alcohol and drugs offer a quick escape by altering one's sense of perception or reality. While high or intoxicated, a person may be able to forget his or her troubles for a short time, until the person detoxifies. Afterward, however, the person has the same worries and loneliness as before, but an increased intensification of these feelings, in addition to guilt and shame for taking the easy way out. In addition, there is a great danger of becoming addicted and dependent on chemicals. However, when orgiastic states are used for transitory satisfaction they often become an accepted routine, and the more they occur, the greater the amount of sex, drugs, or alcohol required to get the same effects.

At first it may take one or two drinks to become intoxicated or one orgasm to help one forget one's troubles and feel relaxed. But over time it takes an increased amount of alcohol and/or drugs and more orgasms to achieve the same sense of pleasure, much in the same way that abuse increases in intensity over time.

When abuse is occurring, it is easy to understand how violence can increase with each failed attempt at solving the problem by using an orgiastic state. Violence itself is an orgiastic state. The more a person experiences feelings of isolation and frustration, the more violence an abuser may choose to use against others. Violence results in an adrenaline rush, which intensifies the effect for the abuser. The adrenaline serves to reinforce the use of violence.

Soon the orgasms, intoxication, and violence are not enough to satisfy the abuser's quest for tension relief. Force becomes more common as a means to release tension and increase the denigration and humiliation of the victim. As the abuser uses drugs and alcohol to cope, he or she soon finds an easy excuse for the violence—blaming it on the drug or alcohol that caused the person to be in an altered state. However, the reality is that drugs and alcohol never make a person behave violently; violence is always a choice. All acts of abuse are planned, and the plan may include using drugs and alcohol to serve as an excuse.

CHAPTER NINE

Factors of Healthy Relationships

Carl Rogers's view of the therapeutic relationship is akin to the makeup of a healthy relationship. Although his four factors are meant to pertain to the therapeutic process, I believe they also shed light on the factors that help make fulfilling personal partnerships. Rogers is the founder of Person Centered Therapy. He believes that therapeutic techniques are not as important or effective as the therapeutic relationship established between therapist and client. This basically means that the therapist's techniques will only be as effective as the therapeutic relationship is strong.

Rogers believes that the most important aspects of any therapeutic relationship are *congruence, empathy, positive regard,* and *unconditional positive regard*. I believe that these are equally important in any personal relationship we enter.

Congruence refers to being genuine at any given moment. An example of this would be if a person were angry but smiling his or her facial expression would not express the person's true feelings of anger. Congruence is allowing oneself to express the real person. Being genuine with emotions and wants requires great risk because an individual may be rejected by a significant other or taken advantage of, even laughed at. However, the only way to be truly genuine is to take the risk of being who one is.

Empathy refers to understanding a significant other's world as accurately as possible. This involves commitment of both time and energy. Listening is the most important skill required to hear the true message given by the significant other. It does not mean that an individual will fully understand the partner's messages or even agree with them, but that one should take the time to listen and ask for clarification when needed. Empathy also involves the ability and willingness to put oneself in the other person's shoes, appreciating what the other is going through and feeling what they are feeling.

Positive regard is treating a significant other in a warm, accepting, positive manner, being supporting and affirming to the significant other. A person enters a relationship to feel needed, wanted, and loved. Positive regard involves letting the significant other be aware of the degree to which one respects, loves, and wants the other.

Unconditional positive regard refers to the ongoing positive feeling a person has toward the significant other without any restrictions. It is unconditional, without any evaluations or limitations. Unconditional positive regard decreases the chance of experiencing disappointment because a person warmly accepts the genuine being of a significant other. It means "I love you" even when one makes mistakes or lets the partner down. It involves expecting honesty, not specific things or feelings.

Healthy relationships are characterized by the presence of several shared factors. It is important to realize that these factors occur with different intensities, and the intensity of each may change over time and with different circumstances and situations. The seventeen factors that help characterize a healthy relationship are:

1. Trust
2. Honesty
3. Openness
4. Communication
5. Understanding
6. Flexibility/Compromise
7. Boundaries
8. Growth
9. Acceptance
10. Respect
11. Intimacy/Spirituality
12. Commitment
13. Space
14. Individuality
15. Affirmations
16. Equality
17. Risks

Each of these factors is necessary, and together they characterize a healthy relationship.

Trust

Trust is an important requirement for any relationship. It involves having confidence in your significant other as well as in yourself. Believing that your significant other is faithful first requires confidence in yourself. Trust refers to reliability and is proven over time. It is an active investment in yourself and in your significant other. Trust requires respect for yourself and your significant other. You must trust that you will be honest and that you will take the risk of being hurt as well as the risk of achieving a healthy relationship.

In most instances in which jealousy occurs, the significant

other had done nothing to deserve such scrutiny. Jealousy indicates two things: the jealous person believes that he or she owns the significant other, and the jealous person is afraid of acting in the way they blame the significant for acting—it is a matter of projection. Projection is the act of transferring qualities that one does not like in oneself and placing them on one's significant other. An example would be if you're falsely accused of being unfaithful, it is likely that your significant other is struggling with his or her own issues of faithfulness. Again, one must first trust oneself; then one can trust one's significant other.

Honesty

Honesty, being genuine, involves a willingness to see oneself and a significant other as each person is, without selectivity. Basically this means that both people are being truthful about their needs, requests, and beliefs and that both attempt to communicate these as directly and genuinely as possible. If one partner is disappointed, he or she should say so. To do otherwise would only serve to deny one an emotion that exists, discrediting one's true feelings.

Before you can honestly see a significant other as the person he or she truly is, you must be able to look in the mirror and see the person you really are, not just the person you want to be. Be as totally honest as possible about your negative and positive qualities.

Honesty also means being genuine, and this means sharing your true emotions through clear, accurate communication at the time they occur. Spontaneity is also part of honesty and refers to reacting to or sharing the moment without planning. Honesty involves much risk.

◆   ◆   ◆

Openness

Openness refers to the willingness of both partners to hear each other's messages and to consider the messages regardless of whether they believe in or agree with what is being communicated. Openness is risk in its raw state. At times a significant other may not like what he or she sees in his or her partner, but honesty, acceptance, flexibility, and love all require openness.

Communication

Communication refers to the skill of receiving and giving messages and may be verbal or non-verbal. Examples of non-verbal communication include facial expressions, body posture, physical proximity, and participation level. If a significant other is not returning the physical intimacy his or her partner desires, the non-verbal message is clear: he or she does not want to be doing whatever it is the partner is doing. All too often we only pay attention to the messages that help us to achieve our wants. But true communication must be genuine, open, and accepted to permit a relationship to grow.

Verbal communication is stating wants and needs and includes actually saying "yes" or "no." It is important to respect disagreements as a healthy part of any relationship. After all, there are three personalities and forces involved in any relationship. Communication is expressing oneself and hearing the messages one's significant other is giving.

Many people become frustrated with silence, mostly due to their own lack of a sense of security. But silences, like behaviors, often speak louder than words. If a spiritual relationship has been established, silences may bring comfort, security, a sense of belonging and union. If you or your significant other comment about communication problems, then take the time to discuss the way you both communicate verbally and non-verbally. It may be in your best interest to take a class on better communication or get into couples therapy to improve communication skills.

Understanding

Understanding a partner takes time and a genuine willingness to truly hear what he or she has to say, including both verbal and nonverbal messages. Understanding involves knowledge of both yourself and your significant other. When unclear about a message, ask for clarification. Although at times it may seem embarrassing to ask for clarification, the minor embarrassment you may experience could possibly lead to an improved understanding of your significant other's message.

Understanding takes patience. However, if you continue not understanding what the other person is saying, you may begin to feel frustrated. Without an understanding of your significant other's messages, you lack understanding of his or her true feelings, wants, needs, and emotions. The bottom line here is to ask about what you don't understand.

Flexibility

Flexibility refers to the ability to bend and compromise, even when you may disagree with what is being asked. Flexibility implies that there may not be a perfect correct answer for every situation. At times, a person simply chooses the option that makes the most sense at that moment. Even if you believe you are right and your significant other is wrong, compromising may be indicative that you care about yourself, your significant other, and the relationship.

But it is important to remember that you do not need to give up your morals and values. Give in only to the degree that you are comfortable with or you may experience resentment and frustration as a consequence.

Boundaries

Boundaries are a vital aspect of any relationship. Remember that a healthy relationship involves a triad; there are three sets of boundaries to which attention must be paid. Boundaries need to be clearly identified to be effective. Boundaries mark where one person or identity ends and where the other begins. Without boundaries, confusion occurs and it then becomes difficult to differentiate where one person ends and the other person begins.

An example of boundary confusion and diffusion is when you are dependent on your significant other to the extent of doing whatever is asked of you, even when you morally disagree with what is being said, even to the extent of giving up your own goals, rights, and dreams. What happens is that you become an extension of your significant other and lose much if not all of your own sense of identity. Also, the relationship will not grow when healthy boundaries do not exist, when two people are intertwined to the point of losing their own identity (see Figure 10).

The result of this occurrence is a single identity instead of two crucial identities that originally made up the foundation of the relationship. It is impossible for the relationship to do anything but stagnate or decline at this point. It is like pulling the foundation out from under a home; the result is that the house tumbles to the ground.

Growth

Remember that a healthy relationship is an ever-changing

process. Growth involves work, commitment, flexibility, and responsibility. Growth is a healthy process even when growing leads to the termination of the relationship. As each person continues to grow, he or she may find that the relationship is not where they want or need it to be. If you or your significant other ends a relationship, it doesn't imply that either of you do not care for or love the other, but rather that one of you is being honest about his or her feelings and may have grown apart.

You can truly love someone yet not be involved in an intimate relation with that person. If you are fortunate, however, you may be able to maintain a friendship. However, at times, a total termination of contact occurs. The point here is best summarized by the saying, "If you love something, set it free. If it comes back, it is yours. If it does not come back, it was not yours in the first place." Despite this, you may feel sad, depressed, or even angry that the relationship has ended.

Respect

Respect is an ongoing concern about the well-being of your significant other. It is important in any relationship and includes acceptance, healthy communication, and risk taking. Respect is making time to truly hear what your significant other is saying, even when you do not like what you hear. It means not assuming meaning, not taking things for granted.

Respect is allowing your significant other to be who the person is and supporting the individual as he or she continues to grow and develop into who or what the person wants to become, allowing for the growth or termination of a relationship.

Acceptance

Acceptance of oneself means allowing for strength and

weakness, to accept reality as it is, and if dissatisfied with reality to make the necessary changes. It is also important to accept your significant other as he or she is. Just as you allow yourself to have strengths and weaknesses, it is imperative that you allow your significant other to have strengths and weaknesses.

Acceptance of termination is also important. If for any reason the relationship needs to end, it is important to accept the termination so that you may move on. Doing so may increase the chance that you may continue to respect yourself and your significant other even after the termination has occurred. Acceptance also includes coming to a mutual agreement as to where the relationship is going, whether it is terminating or growing. The bottom line is to reach an amenable agreement or conclusion. Respect requires a comfort level with yourself, your capabilities, and your limitations. You must be able to confront your own fears, hopes, dreams, and reality.

Trust requires respect. Respect is not taking advantage of your significant other. For example, if he or she is depressed, the person may very much appreciate a hug, being held, and even cuddling. But your significant other may not wish to have sex, to kiss, or even to have you stay with them. Respect means to honor and appreciate your significant other's emotional, physical, sexual, and spiritual well-being and to not take advantage of their limitations.

Respect is a key ingredient to love. Without respect, love cannot exist. Respect of all three parts of the relationship triad is essential.

Intimacy/Spirituality

Intimacy and spirituality refer to a non-spoken, non-verbal union—the warm feelings that being with your significant other brings, the feeling of security whether together or apart. It is somehow knowing what to say, how to touch, or what to do or not to do. Intimacy allows you to bring out the best in your significant other even when the person may outshine or out succeed you.

Intimacy may be social, emotional, sexual, physical, and spiritual. Intimacy is understanding, openness, fondness, affection, love, and tenderness. It is experiencing belonging with another person, a sense of knowledge and deep emotion.

Commitment

Commitment refers to an active investment of yourself given freely to your significant other. It is active because you are required to give of yourself, your time, and your energy and to take risks. It is an active choice because you must decide whether or not to share yourself with another; it does not just happen. Commitment also includes an acceptance of a long-term relationship, including both the good and the bad times.

Commitment requires acceptance, trust, openness, and intimacy/spirituality. Commitment—not only to each other, but to the relationship as well—involves the dedication to stand by each other through the good and bad times, to meet the needs and requests of your significant other without complaining and without compromising your values.

Space

Although a relationship involves two individuals who choose to share their lives together to form one relationship, it is imperative that the individual identities of both be allowed to grow. To expect that your significant other will always want to spend time with you, that the person will drop whatever he or she is doing upon request, is selfish. Space refers to time apart, away from your significant other. Space is healthy, and when intimacy, spirituality, trust, acceptance, and love are present, space brings security not fear.

Space includes having friends, both male and female, who either partner can spend time with. Having different interests, hobbies, and sports without a dating partner is also healthy. If all of one's time is spent with a significant other, then it is likely that the relationship will become smothering and unhealthy.

Individuality

Individuality makes you different and separate from everyone else. Individuality includes boundaries; it is the essence of who we each are. Included here are traits, habits, and the ability to have a separate identity from your significant other. It may also include self-sufficiency. Individuality includes having your own set of male and female friends with whom you can spend time. It also includes the right to set personal goals and limitations. Without individuality a relationship stagnates.

Affirmation

Affirmation refers to the process of validating the significant other as a whole person, even when one dislikes certain qualities or behaviors. This means being appreciative of a person's physical qualities and of who the person is, as well as to acknowledging accomplishments. This can involve positive comments such as "You look nice," "You did a good job," or "You really mean a lot to me." It means doing whatever you feel and believe to make that person aware of the respect and pride one has for the person and to help the person grow as an individual. Giving yourself affirmations is also important.

Equality

Equality refers to maintaining a power balance that allows both people to be the best they can be while maintaining the respect and well-being of each. Equality means not scolding the significant other when he or she displeases the partner, but rather accepting the fact that both people are equal, that both have strengths as well as weaknesses, and that these strengths and weak-nesses can be compatible. In a healthy relationship each person's strengths and weaknesses complement the other's. Equality means that both people have equal power in making decisions and plans; no one person has more power than the other.

Risk

Risk involves revealing vulnerabilities, allowing oneself to be boldly right as well as boldly wrong, and sharing dreams, hopes, aspirations, failures, and successes with the significant other without any guarantee as to how the person will respond.

Risk means investing in the relationship without any guarantees, without ever knowing what the future will hold. Risk is the active process of being open, genuine, honest, and vulnerable. Risk allows us to laugh with, not at, our significant other's strengths, weaknesses, shortcomings, and dreams as well as laughing with and accepting our own.

There are no magical potions or tricks to having a healthy relationship. Healthy relationships also do not occur by chance; they require a lot of work. The work is often not difficult, but even when it is difficult the challenge of building a healthy relationship far outweighs the effort given and sacrifices made. I believe that some factors, however, are core characteristics, and these take an extra effort to establish. The core factors include respect, trust, boundaries, growth, commitment, and love. All of the other factors are in some way connected to these six.

Unhealthy relationships are characterized by the lack of these characteristics or the presence of their opposites. If any type of abuse is occurring, the relationship is unhealthy

Factors in a Healthy Relationship	Factors in an Unhealthy Relationship
Trust	Lacks trust; jealousy may be present.
Honesty, spontaneity	Abuser only sees what he or she wants to see, deceives the significant other and self.
Openness	Closed, private, unwilling to share anything about one's own thoughts, wants, and emotions.
Open communication	Closed, one-sided, unclear messages; also double-bound communication.
Understanding	No effort is made to become aware of the significant other's needs, feelings, wants.
Flexibility/compromise	Inflexible; compromise occurs only when abuser's demands are met, or during honeymoon phase.
Clear boundaries	Unclear, diffuse boundaries, as if both partners are one; victim sacrifices all identity and individuality.
Growth	Stagnation; intimacy becomes a routine chore.
Acceptance of self, partner, and relationship	Little or no acceptance of self, partner, or relationship.
Respect	Belief that one partner is godlike while other is worthless; respect demanded by abuser, but abuser gives none in return.

Factors in a Healthy Relationship	Factors in an Unhealthy Relationship
Intimacy/spirituality	No warm feelings; intimacy is like a chore; fear is present; force may be used.
Commitment is an active choice.	Both partners are committed only to one person's needs; victim feels trapped.
Space	Victim expected to spend all free time with abuser; may give up friends, family, school, job; victim feels isolated.
Individuality	Differences not respected and growth not fostered.
Affirmations	Given only when victim gives in to demands or during honeymoon phase.
Equality, shared power	A one-up, one-down situation; force and coercion are used. Physical, psychological, and sexual violence may occur.
Risks taken by both partners.	Victim afraid to express emotions, wants, or needs for fear of further abuse.

Each of these seventeen factors may occur at its own intensity, and over time certain factors may be present more than others. It is also important to be aware that some healthy factors may be present even in an unhealthy, abusive relationship. Maintaining a good relationship requires an ongoing evaluation of how each person's needs are being met, as well as an effort to ensure that the seventeen factors are present.

Healthy relationships take time to develop, and that is where commitment comes in—a commitment not only to energy and effort but to the significant other as well. Although some people believe that love and the development of a healthy relationship may occur instantaneously, they are only fooling themselves into settling for a relationship that will not produce the strong positive feelings they are hoping for, and such a fast oc-curring relationship will probably not be long-lasting. Love re-quires patience, time, perseverance and a willingness to take many risks.

CHAPTER TEN

Sexual Behavior and Abuse

Just as relationships may be healthy or unhealthy, sexual behavior may also be healthy or unhealthy. All of the factors that help make relationships healthy also apply to healthy sexual contact (see Chapter 9). The most important factor, however, is respect. Before we are capable of loving another person, we must first respect that person. Respect is a necessary factor of love; without respect there can never be love. Healthy sexual behavior demands respect and love. Respect is the factor that most differentiates unhealthy sexual behavior from healthy sexual behavior.

Often people are involved sexually with a significant other before an attempt is made to build a genuine, solid relationship. Solid relationships take time to develop. Although sex may create an illusion of love, all that may exist without a solid relationship is temporary relief from loneliness.

Most people take sexual contact for granted, simply expecting it as a result of dating someone. Most people never fully understand or appreciate the intimacy and spirituality that are an integral part of healthy sexual behavior. Intimacy is the closeness of two people that results from mutual respect, openness, a willingness to grow, and, of course, love. Intimacy is spiritual; it cannot be seen or physically touched but is instead felt or experienced.

Intimacy may include sexual contact, but *sexual contact does not have to be involved.*

As a result of not attempting to establish a solid relationship that involves intimacy and spirituality, many people do not have healthy sexual contact. Many people strive only for physical pleasure or orgasm. When the goal of sexual contact is only to "feel good," then the beauty of sexual intimacy is lost and intimacy and spirituality can not occur. As a result, both people feel empty and far apart, and at least one person may feel used and victimized.

Healthy sexual contact allows both people to make their wants known and to have their wants met. This does not guarantee that our significant other will meet our requests, but rather that both partners will at least have the opportunity to communicate their requests.

In Chapter 1, I defined sexual abuse as any forced sexual contact. Sexual assault covers several different types of sexual violence, including date rape and stranger rape. Date rape refers to a sexual assault or rape that occurs during a date or when the abuser is involved in a dating relationship with the victim (see Figure 4, the Continuum of Force). A person who commits date rape does not care for the victim. Just as all abuse is a planned, conscious choice made by the abuser, sexual assault, date rape, and stranger rape are also planned acts of violence.

Sexual assault does not just happen, as some people believe. All rapes are planned, and the abuser makes the decision to have their demands met without regard for the victim's rights or well-being. It is estimated that in 90 percent of all cases of sexual assault and rape the victim knows the rapist.

There are two types of force that may be used to force people into having sex against their will: psychological and physical. Examples of physical force include forcing another person to be touched on his or her genitals, making the victim touch the abuser's genitals, and any forced penetration. Penetration is the insertion of any object or body part into any body opening; this includes oral, anal, and vaginal penetration.

Physical abuse also occurs here because the abuser physically attacks the victim and forces sexual contact. Physical force may include hitting, restraining, removing the victim's clothing, and performing any sexual act on the victim without consent. The use of physical force as described constitutes date rape.

Many date rapes, however, do not include the use of physical force but rather the use of coercion, or psychological force. Also, it is not just women who are date raped. Men can be coerced and physically forced into being sexual just as women can. Although statistics on the number of males who are date raped are difficult to come by, from my research and counseling I estimate that nearly 30 percent of all victims who experience date rape are male.

Coercion refers to the use of tricks, pressure, or threats to make people perform an act against their will. There are two types of coercion: psychological strategies and threats. Psychological strategies include *intimidation, emotional blackmail, game playing, pressuring, boundary violations,* and *lying.*

Intimidation is the act of causing partners to experience fear for their safety or to doubt whether they are normal or sane. Examples include statements such as "What's wrong with you that you don't want to have sex with me?" "Everyone else is doing it, why don't you?" and "You've got me turned on, and now you have to please me." The goal of intimidation is to make the significant other feel somehow responsible and guilty for the abuser's own sexual arousal, thereby attempting to force or trick the victim into sexual contact.

Emotional blackmail occurs when love and other emotions are used to coerce a dating partner into having sex. Examples include statements such as "If you loved me, you would have sex with me," "I paid for the date, and now you owe me sex," and "Prove that you love me." The goal is to equate sex with love.

Game playing refers to mind games used to get a significant other to give in to sexual demands. Examples include statements such as "If you don't have sex with me, I'll find someone who will" and "I'll stop dating you if you don't." The abuser is using game playing to make the victim believe that the victim is not giving equally to the relationship and that he or she should be giving in to the abuser's demands.

Pressuring refers to the use of nagging, begging, and whining as a way to coerce sex from a partner. Examples may include repeating demands over and over again with words to make the victim feel sorry for the abuser, such as "Come on," and "Please do this for me." These are repeated until the victim gives in to the abuser's demands.

Boundary violations occur when an abuser violates the victim's space and body. The space violations may continue even after the significant other has said "no" or "stop." Examples include removing the abuser's or the significant other's clothing, beginning to have sex without the partner's consent, and refusing to let the victim leave the situation.

Lying refers to the blatant lies that are told by an abuser to get the victim to have sex. Examples include agreeing only to fondle and then going beyond what was agreed upon. The abuser also makes promises to his or her significant other to get sex from the victim, but then refuses to keep or honor the promises made.

These six categories are considered *coercion*.

The second type of force is the use of threats. (Threats were described in Chapter 3.) Again, threats occur any time an abuser warns the victim that the abuser may use force to get sex if the partner refuses to give in to demands. Examples may include threatening to use physical violence, spread rumors, have an affair, or even terminate the relationship. Threats, like psychological strategies, play on the emotions of the victim, especially the emotions of confusion and fear.

The bottom line is that if any of the above types of coercion are used to get sexual contact, date rape has occurred. Most date rapes involve the use of coercion, not physical force. It is important to point out that coercion and physical force may be equally devastating to the victim, and that abusers are aware of what they are doing—committing rape. At the least abusers understand that they are harming and exerting force against their victims. Force does not just occur on its own; individuals have to make a conscious decision to use force. When an abuser talks a victim into doing something the person does not want to do, this is coercion. It is always a conscious choice, and it is always a form of violence.

When a victim is coerced into sexual activity, he or she experiences fear—fear not only of experiencing further physical and sexual harm, but also of losing the person he or she cares about. In this situation, while it is true that a victim can always say no to sexual activity, he or she may be risking further sexual and physical harm by refusing. If given a choice between being physically forced into having sex or allowing the abuser to have sex with a victim as a result of psychological force, the victim may choose to give in and cooperate as a means to avoid further harm. But this is still considered date rape. The victim is not really given a choice; he or she is damned for cooperating and damned for resisting.

I believe that most rape victims are faced with a dual crisis. The first crisis involves actual abuse, rape, or attempted rape. In essence, no matter how it is termed, forced or coerced sex is rape, and there is no justification. Rape is a crime of violence in which sex is used as the weapon. Acts of passion may include kissing, hugging, and other intimate types of behavior, but the key ingredient that differentiates passion from rape is *respect*. Abusers do not listen to or respect the other person's requests and well-being.

The second crisis involves the dilemma of "hating the one you love." When the person expected to love and respect you violates not only your body but also your mind, he or she violates your whole being. Most abusers are more than ready to offer excuses as to why they needed to rape their victims, such as "You got me turned on and I couldn't stop," "I needed to finish once I started," and "You wanted it." These excuses are baseless.

Victims of abuse—whether it is physical or sexual abuse—often attempt to blame themselves for the abusive act. When a person is raped, it is often easier to blame yourself than it is to place the blame on the person you love. The victim makes statements such as "I should have said yes anyway," "He/She is under so much stress that he/she couldn't help it," "I got him/her turned on," or "I need to be less selfish and more giving of myself." Many victims believe that they were raped or physically abused as a result of something they did or did not do, or due to the way they dress or talk. But the truth is that regardless of how a person dresses, talks, or behaves, no one ever deserves or asks to be raped or abused.

Abusers do not decide to rape someone solely on the basis of looks or behaviors, but rather because of the issues of power and control (discussed in Chapter 4) and the desire to humiliate and degrade the victim. Basically this means that an abuser who commits date rape wants to force his or her partner to do something against the victim's will that will result in humiliation and degradation.

Remember that rape is always a conscious choice an abuser makes, and no one causes an abuser to rape someone. Rape is never the victim's fault, ever. Regardless of how much the abuser feels that he or she is being led on, teased, or provoked, it is important to remember that the abuser makes a choice to commit the rape often even before the date begins. All rapes are planned; they never just happen. Abusers do not respect or love their victims; if they did, they would not have forced sexual contact.

Rape is not an act of sexual intimacy, but rather one of power, control, and degradation. It appears much easier to believe this when referring to a stranger rape versus a date rape. When the rape occurs between acquaintances or significant others, it somehow seems less criminal and less important. The hardest, most painful part of being date-raped may be dealing with the fact that without respect, love cannot exist, and therefore the abuser does not love the victim.

One unfortunate way many victims cope with date rape is to block out the experience. Afterward many victims talk of the occurrence as if they were watching someone else, not themselves, being raped. This is called disassociation. Disassociation is a way to mentally escape the pain of being physically and sexually assaulted and is effective for blocking out the bad experience in the short run. However, in the long run it can lead to many problems that may take years to resolve.

A victim is not to blame for abuse. Again, *all* rapes are planned in advance. The abuser plans what will happen, where it will happen, and when it will happen. If drugs or alcohol are used, the abuser plans to use the drugs or alcohol as part of the rape situation.

Healthy sexual behavior always allows both individuals to have power in deciding what type of sexual contact will occur. If people truly respect and love their significant others, they listen to and honor their decision when they say no to sexual contact. Healthy sexual behaviors involve three crucial factors: *consent, respect,* and *intimacy and spirituality.*

Consent

Consent refers to giving permission and agreeing on what will happen. In order for consent to be given:

* The other person must have the right and safety to say yes or no without being forced. This means that the person is not being threatened in any way.
* The person must fully understand what he or she is agreeing to do. It is important that both people speak the same

language, at least somewhat fluently, and are both able to communicate their understanding.

• The person must be in a clear state of mind, that is, not impaired in any way. Impairment would include being under the influence of drugs or alcohol, experiencing mental illness, sleeping, or injured. If somebody has to be under the influence of drugs or alcohol before they will consent to sexual activity, they do not want to have sex. If a person is in any state of physical or mental impairment, he or she is not in a state to legally give consent.

After consent has been given, the next step is to set the sexual boundary, that is, to decide and agree on what type of sexual contact will occur. It is always important to set sexual boundaries in advance when possible. Waiting until the last moment to ask for consent may result in frustration and disappointment. Setting sexual boundaries allows both people to understand what each person would like to share. If you want to fondle or have foreplay but not have intercourse, say so. Agree to only what you feel comfortable doing; remember that it is your right to set sexual boundaries.

Respect

Respect refers to accepting a significant other's boundaries as well as one's own. Also included here is the responsibility for discussing birth control methods and sexually transmitted diseases honestly and openly. If you are close enough to have sex with your significant other, then you are close enough to take the risk of discussing these issues. It is better to experience some embarrassment before engaging in sexual contact then to deal with these issues after finding out that one person contracted a sexually transmitted disease from the other or that pregnancy occurred.

Respect means not taking advantage of a significant other's

physical or emotional state, and it involves watching out for the other person's well-being. If a significant other needs a hug because of being depressed, for example, it is probably not the time to ask for further sexual contact. Putting the other's needs before one's own and being willing to compromise is respect in action.

If you or your significant other changes your mind and decides not to have sex, even after agreeing to or during sexual activity, it is imperative to stop! Everyone has the right to a change of mind, and we all have changed our decisions concerning sexual activities at one time or another. It is a myth that men always want to have sex, or that once sexual behavior has begun, it cannot stop until it is finished.

There is also no such thing as being "out of control" sexually, although many people use this as an excuse to get their partners to continue sexual contact. Once someone states, "stop" or "no," or refuses to participate, it is rape if sexual contact continues. "I don't know," "Maybe," "Not now," "Later," "I'm scared," "Please don't," and "Wait" all should be considered synonymous with "no." When a person refuses to give permission to engage in sexual behavior and the other person begins or continues to engage in sexual contact, rape is occurring.

Respect is putting the needs and best interest of a significant other before one's own, without sacrificing one's own morals and values. If both people cannot agree on sexual boundaries, then it may be time to end the relationship and find others who are more compatible. There are only two types of sex: consensual and forced.

We don't want to disappoint the people we love; we want to please them. But if the sexual contact means more to a significant other than respecting your rights, then the reality is that that person does not love you. It is as simple as that. If a partner cannot accept the fact that no means no, listen to the message being given. If forced sexual contact occurs, it will be exploitative, empty sex. If your significant other physically forces you or coerces you into having sex, that is not an indication of love, passion, or intimacy. It is a clear sign of rape, and rape is violence and abuse.

The relationship of Cindy and Bill is one that resulted in this kind of abuse. When Bill wanted to have sex with Cindy, he often made sure that she had been drinking and was intoxicated. Cindy often refused to have sex with him because she wanted more from their relationship than sex. Bill became angry when she refused him, and he accused her of having sexual affairs with men she knew. Sometimes Bill became sad and told her that he really needed to have sex with her to help him feel better. Sometimes Cindy gave in to his demands and manipulation.

When Cindy had been drinking, she was not able to physically resist Bill as well as when she was sober. She found it more difficult to push him away, and if she wanted to leave, Bill would refuse to drive her home, leaving her stranded and vulnerable. Bill frequently used guilt to make Cindy feel as if she was not giving as much to their relationship. Cindy's friends all agreed that Bill was abusive, but Cindy would not leave him.

In our sessions, Cindy began to identify that after having been manipulated into having sex with Bill that she felt hurt, violated, ill, and used. Bill felt in control, guilty, and satisfied. Unfortunately Bill was not willing to examine his abusiveness any further, and he broke up with Cindy. Cindy continued to learn more about abuse and date rape and chose to continue with therapy. The more she resolved and learned, the stronger she became, and the happier she found herself. She can now set sexual boundaries without feeling trapped or guilty.

Another couple with whom I consulted exhibited a different aspect of abuse. Angie and Dave had been dating a couple of months. Dave complained that she flirted with other men whenever they went out, and that she hinted that she might have sex with other men if he did not satisfy her. Dave cared very much for Angie but sometimes found himself too tired to have sex after work. Angie had trouble accepting his not wanting to have sex.

Angie believed that men are always in the mood for having sex unless they have been cheating. So when Dave said no, she assumed that he was either having an affair or not sexually attracted to her. Angie had manipulated Dave into having sex several times. She made him feel guilty and attacked his masculine image. She would fondle him and lie on top of him while kissing. Even when Dave said no, she continued to seduce him until he gave in or angrily said no.

Dave was having a difficult time with his own sense of masculinity, because he also believed that men should always be ready for sex. He became depressed when he found that he did not always want to have sex with Angie. He also felt extremely sexually and emotionally attracted to her, which further confused him. In our sessions together, both learned about sexuality, dispelling sexual myths, and learned to accept that men, just like women, can say no to sex and are not always in the mood for sex. They managed to grow closer together and continued their relationship.

A third case with which I was involved is a common one on college campuses and high school dating scenes. Adam was a star on the football team at college. Everybody seemed to like him. He was good looking, outgoing, and friendly, and many females wanted to go out with him. He maintained a 3.5 average and frequented the major parties. He asked Kris out on a date, and they planned to go out for pizza and then to a party.

Adam brought her flowers, and they talked all the way to the restaurant. During dinner, they seemed to get along fine, and Kris felt special, knowing that this well-liked man was interested in her; what a self-esteem boost! She felt that she could trust Adam, and agreed to go to the party, which was at his house. There were thirty to fifty people at the party. Everybody was talking and dancing, and the music was loud. Kris and Adam began to drink. Later that night, Adam wanted to take Kris on a tour of the house. She agreed.

When they got to one of the bedrooms, Adam said, "This is my room, and I have something to show you on the dresser." Kris entered the bedroom and Adam closed the door. "Kris, you're so beautiful, and I really like you. I want to see you again." Kris was flattered. Adam told her to sit on the bed. He pulled her to sit down, put his arm around her, and began to kiss her. The kissing was nice, and Kris felt special.

Adam then pushed her down on the bed, got on top of her, and began to take their clothes off. He kissed her hard, preventing her from screaming or telling him to stop. Kris attempted to fight him, but before she could do anything, he was having intercourse with her. Adam was *raping* Kris. Afterward, Adam threatened Kris that if she ever told anyone he would smear her name, give her a bad reputation, and physically hurt her. Then he drove her home.

Kris was scared and confused: How could a popular, well-respected man who seemed so gentle hurt her? She blamed herself. She did not tell anyone. While attending another party with her girlfriends, Adam's friend approached Kris and pulled her to an upstairs bedroom. Adam was there, and they turned off the lights. they called Kris a slut and proceeded to gang rape her. Her screams could not be heard due to the loud music. Her friends found her wandering outside, dazed, and confused. They drove her to the emergency room.

Kris was treated for rape. She received therapy for many months and had to drop out of school. It took time before Kris could label what happened to her as rape and to blame Adam and his friends, not herself. This is a common example of what happens in rapes on campuses and at parties. Kris had every reason to trust Adam, but he took advantage of her trust and traumatized her for life. Finally Kris went to the authorities. Adam was arrested and, in therapy, told of his plan to set her up to be raped.

CHAPTER ELEVEN

Rules for Healthy Problem Resolution

Problems and disagreements occur in every relationship. Every problem and argument has at least two participants. One participant's job may be to argue, and the other may be expected to somehow respond. However, the problem affects both people. If problems are not dealt with promptly and directly, anger, guilt, disappointment, and resentment may not only be experienced but also heightened to such a degree that the relationship begins to deteriorate.

The best solution to dealing with problems is through healthy discussion. Many people choose to refer to "rules for fair fighting." However, using the term "fair fighting" somehow seems to validate violence by supporting the belief that as long as the fighting occurred during a "fair fight," it is somehow condoned. Healthy problem resolution is not fighting but discussion. It involves strict rules, and no one person wins; rather, both people triumph, because when a healthy discussion occurs, the relationship is almost always strengthened.

Some rules for healthy, nonviolent problem resolution follow.

Timing

Choose a time when both you and your significant other have the time, energy, and willingness to engage in the discussion. Allow time not only to discuss the issues, but also to show support afterward.

Use "I" Statements

Take responsibility by owning your thoughts, feelings, and behaviors. Use "I" statements and avoid "you," "us," or "we" when referring to the issue. Taking responsibility can lessen defenses and may encourage both you and your significant other to calm down and show respect and support for each other.

Give and Accept Feedback

If you are unwilling to accept feedback, don't give it! However, be aware that the only way to resolve a conflict while maintaining respect is through clear, open, two-way feedback.

Here and Now

It is important to stick to the present issue. Bringing up other issues, especially old ones, will only confuse the discussion. Specify what issue will be discussed and stick to it. If other issues arise, take a break before discussing the next issue. This will decrease confusion and allow each person to physically and mentally prepare for the next discussion.

◆　◆　◆

No Attacking Your Significant Other

Avoid bringing up issues and problems that neither of you can change. You can never undo something you have done in the past; however, you can deal with current emotions resulting from past behavior. Avoid using your significant other's problems against him or her (depression, illness, childhood abuse, loss and grief, etc.).

Respect

Respect both yourself and your significant other. This includes allowing the other person to finish what he or she wants to say without being interrupted or threatened, as well as allowing for tears, a break from the discussion, and for time-outs.

Hold Hands and Face Each Other at Eye Level

Discuss issues in an optimal setting that allows for good communication to occur. Avoid having the television or radio on or being somewhere where someone may interrupt your discussion. If possible, sit across from each other in chairs at a table, on a couch, or on the floor. This will increase eye contact. Holding hands can add warmth while allowing for a feeling of equality, security, and safety. The goal is to avoid a one-up, one-down setting.

Avoid Sarcasm

Put-downs and jokes have no place in a serious discussion. Sarcasm is not respectful and may result in a premature end of the discussion. Sarcasm may continue to build and breed resentment, placing the relationship in jeopardy.

Never Attempt to Win

Either you both win or you both lose. If your goal is to maintain the relationship, it does not really matter who is right or wrong. Focus on resolving the problem without judgment as to who is right or wrong. Even when you may be right, it is better to compromise at times than to satisfy your ego's need to show your significant other up by winning.

Express Feelings Appropriately

It is important to openly and honestly express your feelings. It is most effective to express your feelings at the time that you are experiencing them. Don't wait for days or weeks; this may result in the intensification of feelings as well as building up resentment, frustration, and anger.

Compromise

Remember, no one is always right or always wrong. Your beliefs may different from your significant other's. Remember that the goal is to maintain the relationship, not to prove who is right or wrong or to put one over the other as in a one-up, one-down relationship. Maintaining a relationship requires that the focus be on compromise, and compromise means bending even when you know you may be right. However, being flexible and compromising does not mean you have to give up your morals or values. Only give in to the point that you are morally comfortable with.

Never Assume Meanings or Intentions

If you are not sure what your significant other is saying, ask. Only through inquiry can you clearly understand what the other person is truly saying. Also, no one can ever know what the other is trying to say or what he or she means without the person telling you.

No Mind Games

If your goal is to remain together, don't play games. No one is less or more powerful than the other. Treat your significant other with respect. Do not prematurely apologize or refuse to take the other's concerns seriously. Falsely giving in results in increased resentment and taller, stronger walls between you. Mind games played by one person are a form of manipulation that serves to put the other person down.

Speak Only for Yourself

You are an expert on yourself while your significant other is an expert on him- or herself. Use "I" statements, avoiding "we," "us," and "you." Speaking for your significant other only serves to devalue his or her feelings and thoughts and teaches the other person that you believe yourself more knowledgeable about the person than he or she is.

Do Not Punish the Other

If you want to engage in an intimate adult relationship, act it. A parent-child relationship may include discipline, but a dating relationship requires equality and maturity in power. It is not one's job to discipline one's significant other. When one feels the urge to punish, one should take a time out and refocus on what the real issue is and what one's role in the issue is. Remember that every argument has at least two participants, and each participant is responsible for the problem to some degree.

Time Out and Termination

If you need to end the discussion before it is finished, set a time to resume it. Avoiding the issue will only exacerbate the problem and increase resentment. Also, check it out with your significant other before ending. Attempt to end the discussion when both of you agree on ending. If you recognize that you are escalating, take a time-out, tell your significant other how long you will be gone, and leave quietly. When you return, ask if the other person is ready to continue the discussion, but only if you know you are ready.

No Violence

There must be trust for issues to be resolved, and violence is the quickest way to destroy any and all trust. Violence and abuse indicate a lack of love, respect, and trust. Even if one of you has hurt the other, violence is never justified, asked for, or deserved. Remember that provocation only challenges a person; it is that person who decides how to act. No one is ever out of control.

Wrap-Up and Discussion

When the discussion is finished, talk about the process. How does it feel to follow these rules? Did you feel hurt, misunderstood, or respected? Regardless of whether the issue was resolved, was the discussion worth it? How was the relationship affected by the discussion? Paying attention to and discussing how the problem-solving process went will not only strengthen the relationship but increase the chance of a healthy discussion happening again.

Reward and Intimacy

At the end of the talk reward yourself and your significant other. Give hugs, shake hands, or whatever form of intimacy is appropriate at the time. This will feel good and increase the likelihood of a healthy discussion occurring again. It will also serve to show your significant other how important he or she really is to you. Even when you know you were wrong, owning what you did or said and taking responsibility for yourself feels great.

These guidelines are offered as a model for healthy problem resolution. No one is perfect, but each person can be respectful even when making a mistake. Keep a copy of these rules nearby so you can use them during a discussion. And remember that no one person wins in a relationship. Either both people win or both people lose.

CHAPTER TWELVE

Grief and Dating Violence

Both victims and abusers of domestic and dating violence experience a sense of loss, and with this come feelings of grief and bereavement.

How Grief Is Experienced

Grief may take many forms, including a state of shock or numbness, general confusion, disturbance of appetite or sleeping patterns, impaired concentration, preoccupation with the lost object or person, and a withdrawal from others and activities. As a result of the ways in which grief may be experienced and expressed, it is easy to understand how grief can often be mistaken for other problems such as depression, eating disorders, or alcohol and drug abuse. Despite the fact that grief shares many characteristics and symptoms with these other problems, there are differences between them.

For example, grief differs from depression in that the mood swings during grief tend to occur within a short time span and are typically from sad to normal. With depression, however, the mood swings tend to last longer. A person suffering from grief will also become increasingly interested in others and activities as the individual copes with the grief, whereas with depression the person's interest in others and activities usually does not improve until the depression subsides or until therapy is sought.

As for guilt, a person experiencing grief usually focuses the guilt on what was done or not done in relation to the lost person, whereas with depression the person usually experiences shame rather than guilt. This shame is usually focused on the person's own self-worth, and the person therefore may believe that he or she is bad or worthless.

Other problems may exist along with grief, and when appropriate several problems may be addressed in therapy simultaneously. However, it is imperative to accurately identify and separate which issues are grief and which are indicative of more serious problems, remembering that grief is a normal reaction to loss. Nevertheless, it is important to deal with grief and loss issues so that they do not continue to impact a victim's or abuser's life. When grief issues are not adequately dealt with, the problems associated with grief (some symptoms were mentioned earlier) may continue for years, resulting in long-term resentment, anger, confusion, fear of abandonment, and lack of trust.

Grief is defined as the normal reaction to a loss expressed through emotions and behaviors. *Bereavement* refers to an internal realization of an external reality and includes loss and mourning; this means that the person realizes and is aware of what has happened. *Loss* refers to a perceived or actual loss, including the loss of a significant other, of rights (being violated), of an object, or of morals, values, or dreams. *Mourning* refers to the process of adapting to loss, the process by which people cope with loss. The mourning process occurs along with bereavement. To adequately deal with and resolve grief issues, one must accept and properly identify the grief and, if necessary, seek therapy to help adjust to the loss and to overcome the problems associated with grief. How a person experiences the bereavement process is related to that person's level of development, past and present experiences, future expectations, and social stressors. Loss affects a person's life in six areas:

1. *Physical Effects:* nightmares, disturbance of appetite and/or sleep patterns, lethargy (lack of energy, hopelessness, etc.), heavy or tight chest, body aches, and restlessness.
2. *Cognitive Effects:* difficulty with concentration; constant thoughts of the lost person, object, rights, safety, or dreams (includes actual, expected, or perceived loss); daydreams and nightmares.
3. *Emotional Effects:* sadness, anger, guilt, shame, loneliness, fatigue, numbness, suicidal thoughts, and depression.
4. *Behavioral Effects:* sleep disturbance (difficulty falling or remaining asleep); appetite disturbance (loss of appetite, binge-purging, or overeating); crying; social withdrawal; avoidance or remainders of lost person, object, dream, or moral; acting out sexually; alcohol and/or drug abuse.
5. *Spiritual Effects:* doubts of a higher power, thoughts of deserving loss as a form of punishment.
6. *Relationship Effects:* decreased communication, decreased desire for intimacy, loss of pleasure from or attraction to significant other, loneliness and emptiness, and boredom or fear of relationships.

Coping with grief is difficult, especially for children. At least 70 percent of the victims of abuse and 90 percent of abusers were abused in some way as children. This is an important fact to keep in mind when trying to help victims and abusers.

According to researchers, children who witness marital violence or discord experience more behavioral and emotional problems than children who have not. The major loss here is the child's right to develop within a supportive and safe environment. Children learn not to trust, do not feel safe, and do not believe that they are valued as anything more than objects. Differences in both emotional and cognitive development between abused and neglected children and normal children are common. This may result in chronic unresolved grief, as well as many other problems.

Thus when children who have experienced abuse become adolescents, the stage may be set so that behaving as an abuser or victim may feel and seem appropriate. This is in part a result of not completing the grieving process for their lost rights, including the rights to be cared for, loved, protected, and safe; to be allowed to grow and safely be seen, heard, and listened to; and to be valued. Children, and adolescents especially, need qualified therapists to help them not only complete the mourning process but also to make sense out of what happened. It is also imperative to help adolescents understand how art, music, and other forms of creativity can be used to express their needs and experiences. Often when children and adolescents are abused or witness abuse, they do not have the language, experience, or skills to deal with the abuse effectively.

Adults may attempt to avoid dealing with loss, as if all of the feelings and other investments surrounding the lost person will just disappear over time. For example, many adults truly believe that if they terminate an abusive relationship, they will somehow forget about it. This only leads to unresolved grief. Memories are never forgotten; a person either deals with them or buries them. If they are buried, they will resurface and create further and deeper problems in the future.

Relationships are also affected by loss in many ways. According to Erickson, some of the common effects include:

- inability to attain genuine intimacy;
- enmeshment (losing oneself in the other, becoming one with the other) or disengagement (distancing from the other, no

investment of energy in the relationship or the other person);
- mutual neediness (overdependence on each other);
- anger used as the main method of communication;
- increase in conflicts and power struggles;
- one person doing the feeling for both;
- strained sexual relationship;
- problems in other relationships (family, friends, etc.).

Any combination of these can strain a relationship, and the result may be a loss of a healthy relationship, of friends, or of a sense of sanity.

The Mourning Process

Once loss occurs, grieving must occur to restore equilibrium and complete the mourning process. Just as a child needs to complete certain tasks for growth and development to occur, adults must also complete the mourning process so as to not impair their own growth and development. According to Worden, mourning is the process of adapting to loss or anticipated loss and involves four steps.

Step 1, whether you are a victim or an abuser, is to accept the reality of the loss, which may include loss of a significant other, of safety, or of dreams. During this step you must overcome the defense of denying that loss has occurred. It is important that you accept the reality that you were abused, or that you have abused your significant other. Often victims will acknowledge that they were abused by a significant other but will minimize and deny the effects and severity of the abuse. Abusers also tend to minimize their abusiveness or the effects of their abuse. But minimizing and denying the actual experience of being abused only serves to cheat you of your right to heal. If you cannot fully accept and appropriately label the violence as abuse, the healing process will be severely hampered or may not occur at all.

Step 2 is to fully experience the pain of grief. The importance of experiencing this pain cannot be overstated. Experiencing dating violence is hurtful, and it can be difficult to allow yourself to accept the hurt. Alcohol, drugs, denial, and avoidance all aid in burying the pain. Yet the pain exists regardless of whether or not you choose to feel it. If delayed, however, the pain will be harder to deal with and may complicate your life by creating other problems that prevent you from completing the grieving process. To deny the pain only serves to cheat yourself of healing.

Step 3 is to adjust to an environment, relationship, and significant other that are not abusive. This requires much work. It can be awkward, frightening, and challenging to experience a relationship based on trust, respect, and love rather than paranoia, fear, and violence. It is important to develop new skills you can use to accomplish the tasks that your significant other once did for you. For example, the abuser may have fulfilled the role of sexual partner, accountant, and decision maker. Now you need to learn how to accomplish these and other tasks on your own.

Step 4 is to withdraw emotional energy and reinvest it in another relationship. This step involves refocusing emotional energy into new relationships and allowing yourself to love again. Self-identity, individualization, and self-love are often lost when abuse occurs, especially when abuse occurs over a long period of time. The goal is to learn about yourself, to focus on yourself, and to expand and enhance friendships for support. This does not mean to forget about the other person, but rather to invest energy in other relationships. Remember that most abusers also have a nice, loving side, and despite the abuse some pleasant memories may remain. It is important that you not devalue positive memories; they may hold a special place in your heart and may explain why you cared for the abuser.

Reinvesting emotional energy into a nonabusive dating

relationship can be emotionally rewarding for a victim. Abusers who experience their own pain learn to deal with problems in healthy ways while allowing them to feel whole again as well.

The Effects of Loss on Society and Individual Development

Now we can examine how loss affects society and individual development. Victims of any kind of violence experience loss in one form or another. This loss is generally not dealt with or recognized. Common feelings experienced as a result of loss include shame, guilt, anger, and fear, as well as a distorted thinking process. These are all pertinent to dating violence because victims experience these same feelings. Yet few people help victims overcome the loss they experience. Therefore, the grieving process is rarely completed.

Society teaches men and women how to behave by setting certain expectations. Culturally, men are often taught to be leaders, to achieve, and to be in control. Men are often taught at a young age not to cry, not to show emotions, and not to be submissive in relationships. What is lost here is a very vital aspect of any person: the license to show loving, caring, gentle feelings. But this is not all; for example, the dream of experiencing a relationship which is based on trust, respect, and love is lost when abuse occurs.

Women are often taught to be submissive, to give care, and to be obedient. According to such researchers as Smith, as a result of such values and teachings of society, being abused may be a consequence of or part of female development. Some of the losses experienced by women include the loss of freedom, individuality, intimacy, and dreams. Many women also give up the power to freely express themselves, to have their own needs met (because of the expectation that they should give care), and to have control and ownership of their bodies.

Although these are often thought of as old standards, they are very much alive today, especially within some religious communities and cultures. In some cultures there still exists a misbelief that it is all right for a man to physically, sexually, and verbally abuse his wife. This has carried over into the dating relationship, and, as a result, dating violence occurs. Dobash and Dobash found that most violent acts begin with a verbal confrontation, followed by attempts by women to avoid violence, and finally the physical attack. What is lost here is a sense of safety and security, as well as peace of mind. There is a dwindling sense of power as the victim's attempts to defuse the violence fail. This is one example that indicates the loss of power and control the victim experiences from both the abusive situation and the abuser. Both men and women may experience any of these losses.

The effects of violence on children and adults are manifold. Unfortunately, there are large information gaps pertaining to the issues of loss and grief. I believe that victims and abusers experience continued loss and that this loss is rarely identified or validated. The result is that the mourning process is rarely completed, and therefore grief is ignored.

Types of Loss Experienced by Victims

There are ten main areas of loss in dating and domestic violence: *intimidation, threats, isolation, male privilege, emotional objectification, sexual, using children, economic,* and *physical.* In each of these areas, the abuser may also experience similar losses to the victim.

Intimidation occurs when the victim experiences any form of fear. This occurs through certain behaviors, verbalizations, throwing objects, breaking objects important to the victim, or with looks, stares, or posture. This entails a loss of safety, security, and respect.

Threats may include suicidal threats or attempts, physical harm, and even to spread rumors. Loss of power is present, along with the loss of having to be responsible only for oneself; caretaking is requested overtly and covertly by the abuser. Anxiety occurs, which results from the loss of security and certainty.

Isolation occurs when one person exerts control over the other. This includes deciding what the victim does, who the victim sees, and how the victim's time is spent. Loss occurs because the victim is no longer able to exert autonomy, thereby becoming a puppet. As a result of being isolated from others, the victim loses the right to desperately needed supportive relationships.

The *male privilege* includes traditional, stereotypical rules and roles of how each person is expected to act, which may be due to cultural or religious beliefs. The victim experiences the loss of rights, feelings, trust, and individuality. Because of this belief, the male has the final word, and his needs come first.

Emotional abuse includes all of the "mind games" that abusers play. This includes calling a significant other vulgar names, putting the victim down, or causing the victim to feel worthless. There is a loss of self-esteem and self-worth, the right to feel good about oneself and freedom to actively pursue one's wishes due to lack of faith and confidence in oneself.

Objectification is the belief that a significant other is an object rather than a person. The primary loss is of the victim's right to be treated as a person who has an identity separate from the significant other, rather than simply an extension of the significant other or an object the abuser owns.

Sexual abuse refers to any forced sexual contact. This includes forcing a significant other to perform any sexual activity against his or her will and forcing the person to do anything which may cause injury (psychological or physical). Treating the person as a sex object is also abuse. Losses occurring here include loss of pleasure and trust in sexual activities, loss of the right to say no and not have one's body touched, invaded, or injured, and the loss of ownership of that body.

If there is a child involved (whether from a previous marriage, another relationship, or the present relationship), the child may be used to manipulate the victim. An example of *using children* would be an abuser threatening to harm the parent in the child's presence or to perform sexual acts in front of the child. This blackmail creates the loss of power and control and results in the victim feeling helpless, worthless, and betrayed. The child becomes an object and therefore loses any sense of value.

Economic abuse involves controlling how money is spent and even overtly taking money from a significant other. This occurs when an abuser demands that the significant other buy things, pay for the abuser's bills, or pay for the expenses incurred on a date. Loss here includes the postponement of dreams (education, vacation, new car) and feelings of worthlessness.

Physical abuse refers to any attack made against a person's body, either with a weapon, object, or body part. Loss here is comprehensive, because it involves most of the types of loss mentioned before. There is a loss of physical safety, a sense of sanity, and dignity. As a result the victim may be unable to relax, having to always be vigilant of the abuser for fear of further abuse.

These are only a few examples of how grief results from dating violence. There is a great need to address grief and loss issues when involved in an abusive dating relationship. Abusers and victims who are involved in an abusive relationship or marriage experience much loss, thereby necessitating the bereavement process. Yet frequently people do not look at the losses incurred in an abusive relationship. Further research into this area is needed. Professionals need to see that both victims and perpetrators of abuse must learn to deal with the resulting issues of loss if they are to become part of healthy relationships in the future.

CHAPTER THIRTEEN

Healing from Dating Violence

When dating violence has occurred, it is imperative that the victim and abuser receive help so that they may recover from the effects of abuse. Many people believe that simply ending an abusive relationship will end their problems and that they will not be affected any longer once the relationship has ended. This will never work for abusers; it may work for some victims, but most victims will continue to experience some problems in future relationships.

Reality has shown that abuse can affect a person's life physically, emotionally, cognitively, sexually, and spiritually. It is important to remember that memories can never be forgotten or erased, no matter how hard a person tries. If an individual buries them, they will find some way to resurface later.

Some people believe that once a person is a victim or abuser, he or she will *always* be a victim or abuser. This is a myth. People can and do recover from the effects of abuse. The way most people get stuck, however, is by keeping the abuse a secret and refusing to receive help.

People maintain the secret of abuse when they accept the blame for their significant others' behavior. Most often it is the victim who does this, somehow believing that he or she is responsible for having been abused. But no one can ever cause a person to abuse another, just as a person can never cause someone to change. It is the *abuser's choice* to be violent and the *abuser's choice* to receive or not to receive help. Another way to keep abuse secret is to bury the problem by denial or by alcohol or drug use. The more a person runs away from a problem, however, the longer the person will remain trapped in the role of victim or abuser, because no one can heal until one openly chooses to deal with the problem.

Unfortunately, when most abusers and victims begin to receive help, they often do not follow through with their commitments to change. Many abusers, for example, seek therapy and education only after they are ordered by the courts to do so. When people do not seek help on their own initiatives but rather as a result of the courts, it decreases the chance that long-term change will occur.

However, for those motivated to change, there are several options for both abusers and victims to overcome their abuse experiences. The options include *support groups, individual therapy, group therapy,* and *couples therapy.*

Support groups offer a safe environment to express emotions, share histories, and receive support from others who have similar experiences. The goal of such groups is to provide information, encouragement, and backing. This is accomplished by education about abuse and coping with abuse and through peer support. The goal of a support group is not to change behavior but to offer encouragement and support for changes that have been made or are in the process of being made. Usually members will be involved in individual or group therapy while in the support group.

I caution victims and abusers to avoid using any twelve-step support group for dealing with the issues of abuse. Twelve-step groups are not designed to address issues other than what those specified—chemical dependency, sexual addiction, or eating disorders. In fact, these groups can often worsen an abuser's or victim's situation because of the helpless and powerless role people assume they are in. There is no proof that twelve-step groups are effective or helpful when dealing with abuse issues, which they were not designed to deal with.

Support groups are most often facilitated by volunteers who have experienced abuse themselves. Most have received some training although the amount and quality of training, varies greatly. Participation in support groups usually last two to twelve months, although some people attend for years.

Individual therapy involves meeting with a therapist alone. The primary advantage is that the person can receive individualized attention and may also be able to deal with other issues as they occur. Individual therapy offers the chance to identify specific issues, prepares the person for other therapy (group, couples, or family), and allows the opportunity to practice and improve communication skills and other new behaviors without others present.

Most often the therapist will have a master's degree, sometimes a Ph.D., in psychology or social work. I do not recommend entering into therapy with anyone who does not at least hold a master's degree and is licensed as a psychologist or clinical social worker; the issues surrounding dating and domestic violence are extremely complex and require a therapist trained in abuse issues and other mental health issues. It may take three to twelve sessions before therapy appears to be working. At that point a client should be seeing changes and feeling supported. If not, the client may need to find a different therapist. The reasons a therapist may not be right for an individual include a client not being ready for therapy, the therapist's style not fitting, or the therapist not having expertise in working with abuse issues. Individual therapy is most effective when group therapy is occurring as well.

Group therapy offers the opportunity, under the guidance of a qualified therapist, to share experiences with others who have also been involved in abusive relationships. There are separate groups for abusers and victims. The goal of group therapy is to change behavior through education, role-playing, and in-depth processing of issues. The difference between support groups and group therapy is that support groups are not effective in changing behavior but do strengthen changes that occur in therapy. Group therapy works on changing behaviors with the guidance of a trained therapist, offering more structure than a support group.

Group therapy has the advantage of drawing on the experiences and knowledge of all of the group members. Change often occurs when a group member gains insight or changes his or her behavior. This change also affects the other group members, who were in part responsible for encouraging and supporting the changes that occurred.

When the group is cohesive and strong, everyone takes an active role in confronting, supporting, and guiding the other members. All can offer feedback while remaining focused on their own issues. Group therapy is the treatment of choice for both victims and abusers of dating and domestic violence. Much more change can take place within a shorter amount of time with group therapy.

Group therapy lasts approximately six to twenty-four months. Again, the same rule of time applies here as stated before: If after three months you are not seeing some change or feeling helped, seek a different group. Again, individual and group therapy together are the most effective regimen for treating abuse issues.

Couples therapy offers the victim and the abuser who want to remain together a chance to heal together; it is a prerequisite to rebuilding the relationship. However, for couples therapy to be safe and effective in abuse situations, it must not occur until both the victim and the abuser have completed their own individual and group therapies or are far enough along in their therapy to safely attend couples groups. Both the abuser and the victim should be encouraged to continue in their support groups. If couples therapy is begun before both have completed their own healing processes, abuse is likely to continue. This is because the couple is not ready to openly discuss their issues until they have identified their issues, taken responsibility for their behaviors, have significantly modified their problem behaviors, and are willing to calmly deal with these issues. In most cases, however, couples terminate their relationships before therapy has begun, mostly due to the lack of trust and the difficulty involved in guaranteeing the safety of the victim. Successful couples therapy may last approximately three to twelve sessions.

Individual and group therapy, as well as support groups, should be focused on the short term. Remember that a person who chooses to terminate therapy or support groups may return at a later time, and I believe that people who experience abuse need time away from the support group and therapy to find out what has worked, what they have learned, and what else they would like to change. They can then decide if they need further help to accomplish their goals or whether they can fulfill them on their own.

Unfortunately, if a victim remains involved in a support group or therapy longer than necessary, the group and therapy may revictimize them. Many group facilitators and therapists keep people involved in therapy or support groups longer than clinically necessary, and as a result prevent them from making the changes the clients wanted or needed to make.

This occurs when the therapist or facilitator begins to become a caretaker for the person treated, overprotects him or her, or becomes over-empathetic, or when the therapist dislikes the client. Such an impasse can be identified when the therapist or facilitator refuses to let the client move on into the next phase of therapy or refuses to support the person's decision to terminate therapy. When any of these situations occurs or when the abuser or victim is not encouraged to take risks or to practice their new behavior changes, it is imperative that the client terminate therapy with that therapist.

One last problem that can occur is when the therapist or facilitator becomes friends with the victim or abuser, stepping out of the professional role into a more causal, social role. The reality is that once the therapist or facilitator has worked with a person in a professional role, whether in a support group or therapy setting, there should never be a social relationship with the client. Professional, ethical, and legal guidelines prohibit this conduct and refer to this as a *dual relationship*.

Social and romantic relationships are not allowed because of the power the therapist or counselor has over the client, as well as the fact that when the two met, the abuser or victim was vulnerable. If such contact occurs or is asked for or hinted at by the professional, the client should report the therapist to the psychology or social work licensing board or the state attorney general's office. If this professional is harming one person, he or she is probably harming other clients as well.

The Healing Process

Ending a violent dating relationship involves several steps. The first step is to acknowledge the problem. No problem will go away by being ignored. Admit what is happening as honestly as possible. Remember that the victim is never to blame for being abused. It is imperative that the abuser admit to his or her problem in order to change. It is impossible to change when either person has not identified the problem.

Step two is admitting responsibility for one's own actions. No one is perfect; we all make mistakes, but no mistake ever justifies being abusive. Put the blame where it belongs—with the abuser. The only person each of us can ever be responsible for is oneself.

Taking back that power can be energizing and calming. If you are a victim, stop accepting responsibility for your abuser's behavior. It is important for the abuser to accept full responsibility for his or her violent behavior and stop rationalizing and justifying the abuse.

Step three is to restore the self-pride and self-esteem that abuse has taken away. Both victim and abuser lose self-esteem and pride when abuse occurs—the victim as a result of being degraded, abused, and violated as a human being, and the abuser when he or she chooses to use violence against a significant other as a way to have needs met. Both the victim and abuser are capable of restoring their own pride and esteem.

Step four is to follow through with all commitments. For victims to learn how to break out of the victim role takes time and effort. Victims may remain in the victim role until they learn not to accept anything less than respectful, caring relationships. In most instances it is the abuser who fails to follow through on commitments. Most abusers who begin therapy do not continue long enough to benefit in the long run. For long-lasting change, both victim and abuser need to understand that change does not come easily. Learning not to abuse or be abused takes more than just a promise to change.

Healing from abuse takes patience and commitment. Change occurs over time, and it involves much work. The primary goal for victims is to learn that they are not at fault for the abuse—it was the abuser's fault. Rebuilding the victim's self-esteem and confidence is the next step. The final step is learning not to allow others to abuse one and how to protect oneself should it happen again. The best protection is prevention, and this includes the protection plan in Appendix V.

The victim has the power to remain in or leave an abusive

relationship. It is the victim's choice, and it is imperative that he or she gain this understanding and self-empowerment. If the victim chooses to remain in an abusive relationship, however, in no way does it justify the person being victimized or place the blame on the victim. In therapy, the victims become aware that they have the power to make decisions. It is not always possible to prevent an abusive incident from happening, but knowing what to do if it does happen gives the victim power to protect him- or herself from further abuse and offers the person the opportunity to take legal action against the abuser.

The primary goals for abusers are to learn what constitutes abuse and to stop abusing their victims and others. It is important for abusers to pay special attention to the cue areas so that they will know when they are escalating. When escalation occurs, abusers can choose to remove themselves from the situation and release their tension by exercising, meditating, or performing some other activity. In order to move on, abusers must accept that they are 100% responsible for their abusive behaviors and that no one ever causes them to behave violently. Understanding that provocation does not cause or justify violence is extremely important.

If an abuser is going to change his or her abusive tendencies permanently, a commitment to change must occur. This involves a significant amount of work, patience, and risk. The abuser may also have other serious problems, such as mental illness or alcohol or drug dependency, that may require additional treatment. Learning and believing that there are no excuses for the occurrence of violence is essential. Violence is always a choice, and the abuser is always in control.

One of the hardest things for an abuser to do is to find support groups to attend. Most support groups are for victims only. Yet support groups could be important for abusers, too. If a formal support group for abusers is not available, it may be necessary to find another type of support group to attend. Without ongoing support for at least six to twelve months after the completion of therapy, the victim and abuser may find it difficult to maintain their behavior changes. This lack of support does not in any way justify abuse recurring, but rather places an extra burden on finding an appropriate support network.

Most abusive dating relationships end long before the healing process begins. This is due to the fact that most people, especially abusers, fail to follow through on their therapy or fail to make therapy and change a priority. Only qualified mental health professionals can offer the appropriate help to allow both victim and abuser to recover from an abusive personal relationship. Because abuse always becomes increasingly violent over time, it is imperative that both victim and abuser receive the appropriate help they need. The negative effect of people failing to complete therapy is that they may believe that the other person had problems—not them—and that they do not have to make any changes. However, both victims and abusers need to change. If people do not take care of the underlying issues of abuse, but only deal with the symptoms, the problem of abuse will perpetuate itself.

Appendices

Characteristics of Abusers

1. May have intense, dependent relationships with their victims.
2. May be jealous and possessive of their significant others.
3. Lose temper easily, often overreacting.
4. May be generally impulsive.
5. Tend to minimize and deny that they have a problem with violence.
6. Behave violently toward significant others, pets, or objects.
7. Experiences difficulty identifying and expressing emotions other than jealousy, anger, and hostility.
8. May behave violently toward others.
9. May abuse alcohol and/or drugs and may use this to justify their violence.
10. May have dual personality ("Jekyll & Hyde").
11. May have been abused themselves or observed others being abused.
12. Rigid and dichotomous thinking.
13. Expect their significant others to spend most or all free time with them, and to report where they have been.
14. May have stereotypical ideas of how men and women should act.
15. Extremes in behaviors and moods (quick to anger, overdoes

nice things, overly cruel, etc.).
16. May have many friends, be well liked by others, and may even have special talents.
17. May use weapons for protection or to abuse others.

Characteristics of Victims

1. May fear significant others' temper.
2. May attempt to avoid conflicts and disagreements at any cost.
3. Changes in behavior, becoming increasingly withdrawn, aggressive, or vigilant of significant other' presence.
4. Changes in mood, becoming increasingly depressed, anxious, irritable, or even angry.
5. May experience disrupted eating or sleeping patterns.
6. May use and abuse drugs or alcohol in an attempt to numb reality of being abused.
7. May have poor self-esteem and a poor self-image.
8. May have physical injuries, evidenced by marks, scars, and bruises.
9. May behave differently around their significant others than around friends, co-workers, and family members.
10. May have disrupted concentration.
11. May avoid friends or terminate relationships to avoid anyone finding out about the abuse.
12. May have suicidal thoughts or may have attempted suicide.
13. May have self-mutilations, such as tattooing, cutting, or burning.
14. May exhibit extremes in behavior, such as promiscuity,

prostitution, stealing, and reckless behaviors.
15. May avoid discussing their relationships or abusers.
16. May take the blame for the abuse.
17. May spend all free time with their significant others/abusers.
18. May insist on getting permission from their significant others/abusers before making any plans.
19. May experience physical problems such as headaches, nausea, and stress-related problems.

Characteristics of an Abusive Relationship

1. The couple may avoid being around others, often staying home or going out alone rather than in groups.
2. One person appears to do the decision making for both people.
3. Both people may avoid discussing how the relationship is going or may focus only on the good qualities, avoiding discussing problem areas.
4. One person may be scape-goated and blamed for causing all of the problems.
5. Abuse, such as yelling as name calling, may be openly observed and marks or bruises may be noticed on one person.
6. One person may exhibit jealousy toward the other or may accuse the other of infidelity.
7. The couple openly experiences intense and sometimes violent arguments.
8. One person attempts to isolate the other from others and may even sabotage friendships to prevent the significant other from receiving support.
9. One person may be quiet and not call attention to self unless

told to do so by the significant other.

10. Communication appears unhealthy, ineffective, and one-sided.

11. One person may begin to do something that the other person clearly does not want to do, such as engaging in sexual behavior.

Reasons Victims Remain in Abusive Relationships

1. Belief that they can change their abusers' behaviors.
2. Feelings of need for a significant other.
3. Fear for safety, of not being believed, of being alone.
4. May have been taught that abuse is normal.
5. Feelings of guilt, shame, and confusion.
6. Lack of a support system.
7. Belief that they deserve to be abused.
8. Belief that abuse is a sign of passion or love.
9. Denial or minimization.
10. Do not know where to get help or what their legal rights are.
11. May not trust that others will believe or help them.
12. Feelings of hopelessness, frustration, and embarrassment.
13. Belief that they, not their abusers, are crazy.
14. Fear possible effects on their children.
15. Abusers may also be warm and caring at times.

Victim's Protection Plan

During times of crisis it is often difficult to concentrate, and all available options for self-protection may not be obvious. A protection plan allows the victim to follow a set of instructions that allow for maximum safety. The following is an outline for a protection plan.

1. Prearrange a place to go that is safe. This may be with friends, relatives, or even a hotel.
2. Have the following packed and in a place that is accessible, such as in the car, closet, at work, or with friends:

   • clothes
   • money, check book, charge cards
   • important papers such as restraining orders, order for protection, birth certificate, etc.
   • phone numbers of friends, shelters, counselors, etc..

If the protection plan is put in writing, it will be easier to follow during times of crisis. It is also important to pay attention to the abuser's cues, which will alert the victim to the abuser's escalation. The cue areas to watch for are listed below.

1. *Physical/Behavioral*: Be aware of when the abuser's body begins to show signs of increased arousal and stress (escalation stage). Signs of physical escalation may include headaches, a red face, squinting eyes, pacing, clenching teeth and/or fists, yelling, name calling, slamming doors, and hitting things.

2. *Thoughts/Cognitions:* When the abuser begins to rationalize and/or attempt to justify their behavior, they are probably escalating. The abuser may hold beliefs that the victim is an object which belongs to them (objectification), or that the victim may have been unfaithful (jealousy).

3. *Emotional*: When the abuser is focusing on anger and jealousy, they are probably escalating. Often abusers have difficulty identifying or expressing emotions other than anger and jealousy.

4. *Situations*: Most abusers have a difficult time discussing certain topics. When a situation or topic arises which generally turns into an arguement or even abuse, it a good time to leave the situation if possible.

5. *Red Flag Words and Phrases:* These are words and phrases that generally lead into escalation. Included here would be obscene and irritating names, nicknames, and comments about a person's abilities or disabilities.

When any of these cues are present, it is advisable to leave the situation if possible. It is of no use to discuss problems with someone who is escalating; he or she will only hear what he or she wants to hear.

Dating Rights

1. I have the right to refuse a date without feeling guilty.
2. I have the right to ask for a date without being crushed if the answer is no.
3. I have the right to choose to go somewhere alone without having to pair up with someone.
4. I have the right to not act macho or seductive.
5. I have the right to say no to physical closeness.
6. I have the right to say, "I want to know you better before I become more involved or before we have sex."
7. I have the right to say, "I don't want to be in this relationship any longer."
8. I have the right to an equal relationship with the opposite sex.
9. I have the right not to be abused physically, sexually, or emotionally.
10. I have the right to change my life goals whenever I want.
11. I have the right to have friends, including those of the opposite sex.
12. I have the right to express my feelings.
13. I have the right to set limits, to say yes or no, and to change my mind if I so choose, without permission from anyone else.
14. I have the right to stop doing something, even in the middle

of it.

15. I have the right to have my morals, values, and beliefs respected.
16. I have the right to say, "I love you," without having sex.
17. I have the right to be myself, even if it is different from the norm or from what someone else wants me to be.
18. I have the right to say, "I don't want to please you at this time."
19. I have the right to talk with others about my relationships.
20. I have the right to be as open or as closed as I feel comfortable being.

Dating rights 1-10 were adapted from Family Violence Network, Lake Elmo, MN, (612) 770-8544. Reprinted with permission.

References

Corey, F. (1977). *Theory and practice of counseling and psychotherapy (2nd ed.).* Belmont, CA: Wadsworth.

Dobash, R. E., and Dobash, R. P. (1984). The nature and antecedents of violent events. *British Journal of Criminology, 24.* (From *Psychological Abstracts,* 1985, *72* (4), Abstract No. 14778).

Ellis, A., and Harper, R. A. (1975). *A new guide to rational living.* Englewood Cliffs, NJ: Prentice-Hall.

Erickson, B. M. (1986, Oct. 18). Clinical issues related to loss and bereavement. *St. Mary's College, 11.*

Fromm, E. (1956). *The art of loving.* New York: Harper & Row.

Harmon, R. J., Morgan, G. A., and Glicken, A. P. (1984). Continuities and discontinuities in affective and cognitive-motivational development. *Child Abuse and Neglect, 8* (2), 156-167. (From *Psychological Abstracts,* 1985, *72* (7). Abstract No. 9106).

Hershorn, M., and Rosenbaum, A. (1985). Children of marital violence: A closer look at the unintended victims. *American Journal of Orthopsychiatry, 55* (2). (From *Psychological Abstracts,* 1985, *72* (7). Abstract No. 20395).

Johnson, S. A. (1992). *Man to man: When your partner says no.* Vermont: Safer Society Press.

Levy, B. (1984, May/June). Dating violence. *Networker.*

Makepeace, J. (1981, July/August). Premarital violence: Battering on college campuses. *Responses to Violence in the Family, 4* (6).

Smith, S. (1984). The battered woman: A consequence of female development. *Women and Therapy, 3* (2), 3-9. (From *Psychological Abstracts,* 1985, *72* (4), Abstract No. 9808).

Walen, S. R., DiGiuseppe, R., and Wessler, R. L. (1980). *A practitioner's guide to rational emotive therapy.* New York: Oxford University Press.

Walker, L. (1979). *The battered woman.* New York: Harper & Row.

Worden, J. M. (1982). *Grief counseling and grief therapy.* New York: Springer, pp. 7-17.

Index